Caribbean Connections

Jamaica

EDITED BY
Catherine A. Sunshine and
Deborah Menkart

LESSON PLANS BY
Catherine A. Sunshine and
Erland Zygmuntowicz

Ecumenical Program on Central America and the Caribbean (EPICA)
1470 Irving Street, NW
Washington, DC 20010
(202) 332-0292, fax (202) 332-1184
epica@igc.org
www.igc.org/epica

Network of Educators on the Americas (NECA)
PO Box 73038
Washington, DC 20056
(202) 238-2379 or 429-0137, fax (202) 238-2378
necadc@aol.com
www.teachingforchange.org

Introductions and lesson plans © 1991 by the Ecumenical Program on Central America and the Caribbean (EPICA) and the Network of Educators on the Americas (NECA).

Readings are separately copyrighted (see acknowledgements).

Book designs by Melanie Guste, RSCJ, The Center for Educational Design and Communication.

Library of Congress Catalog Number: 90-063270
ISBN: 1-878554-05-0

Printed in the United States of America.

Contents

Introduction

A RETIRED COUPLE FROM OHIO tap their meager savings for a three-day cruise to the Bahamas. Shirts sold in a Dallas department store carry labels saying "Made in the Dominican Republic." Grocery stores a mile from the White House stock hard-dough bread, coconut tarts and ginger beer for the community of 30,000 Jamaicans living in and around Washington, DC.

The Caribbean, along with Mexico, is the Third World region closest to the United States. Its history is intertwined with ours in a multitude of ways. Thousands of Americans visit the islands each year as tourists. Persons of Caribbean origin make up one of the largest immigrant groups in the United States and Canada, and their number is growing. Extensive aid, trade and investment link the U.S. to the Caribbean economically. And the United States has intervened repeatedly in the region to influence political change.

Despite these close links, most Americans know little about Caribbean societies. The region is often depicted as a vacation playground—a paradise of "sun, sea and sand" for the enjoyment of tourists, but not a place where real people live and work. Political and cultural developments in the region often go unreported in the U.S. media. When the Caribbean is discussed, racist and anti-communist stereotypes often blur the images.

As a result, many Americans have missed the opportunity to know the proud history and rich cultural traditions of this neighboring region. Caribbean people have overcome many obstacles and realized outstanding achievements in political, economic and cultural life. The mingling of diverse peoples has produced vibrant and creative cultures, which have enriched U.S. and Canadian societies through the migration of Caribbean people north.

Until recently, most school curricula in the United States included little information on the Caribbean. Textbooks often mention the region in passing during discussion of Latin America. There are few secondary-level resources widely available in the U.S. which are up-to-date, historically and culturally accurate, and which view Caribbean realities through Caribbean eyes.

These books were prepared to enable schools to begin incorporating material on the Caribbean into existing curricula. They are not a substitute for developing curriculum units on the Caribbean, a project which remains to be done. It is hoped that they will help spark interest in teaching and learning about the Caribbean, which will lead to the development of more comprehensive teaching resources.

▼ Objectives and Methods

Four aims guided the editors in their selection and presentation of materials:

• To show Caribbean history and contemporary realities through the eyes of ordinary people, both real and fictional. Oral histories, interviews and other forms of first-person testimony provide a people-centered view of Caribbean life. An example is the autobiographical essay by Leonard Barrett, "African Roots of My Jamaican Heritage" [Unit 2], in which the author recalls the traditions of the community in which he was raised.

• To promote critical thinking rather than simply the memorization of information. All writing contains a point of view, which may be stated or implied. If students examine values and unstated assumptions in whatever they read, they become active participants in their own learning. Where a topic is controversial, we have attempted to include several viewpoints. The student is asked to weigh the evidence, and perhaps to do further research, before drawing his or her own conclusions.

• To stimulate students' interest by creatively combining different types of materials, such as short stories, novel excerpts, non-fiction essays, interviews, newspaper clippings, song lyrics, poetry and drama. Unit 3, for instance, includes an excerpt from a speech by Marcus Garvey, personal testimonies by Jamaicans and Americans who remember Garvey's movement, and a passage from a novel showing the impact of Garvey's movement on Jamaican life.

• To ensure the authenticity and relevance of the material. We sought suggestions from Caribbean people and organizations in the Caribbean, the U.S. and Canada, and relied on an advisory council of Caribbean scholars for ongoing review. There are hundreds of Caribbean civic organizations, and many academics and teachers of Caribbean origin, in North America; they can serve as a primary resource for developing a program of study on the region.

▼ How to Use
These Materials

This book is one of six in the Caribbean Connections series. It is aimed principally at grades nine through twelve, but may be adapted for use at higher and lower levels. The readings, discussion questions and

suggested activities are intentionally varied in their level of difficulty. The instructor is encouraged to select those parts for which the content and level are compatible with curricula in use.

The collection begins with a brief history of Jamaica, which provides a framework for the seven units which follow. Each unit includes a lesson plan, an introduction, and one or more readings. The lesson plans are for the instructor's use; they include objectives, discussion questions and suggested activities. The introductions set the context for the readings; they may be handed out to students, or the instructor may present the information orally. The readings are intended as student handouts.

Each unit also suggests resources for further study. Although varied in difficulty, these tend to be at a higher reading level than the readings included here. They will be particularly appropriate for assigning special research projects to individual students or small groups. Publishers' addresses are included in an appendix.

It is important to note that these materials are not a curriculum, that is, a self-contained program of study. They do not attempt to provide a complete introduction to the Caribbean or to individual Caribbean countries. They present, instead, materials which can be used to supplement curricula in areas such as Social Studies, English

or Third World literature, African-American or Latin American history, Spanish, Multicultural Studies or Global Education. If an instructor wants to devote a full unit of study to the Caribbean or to a certain country, we recommend that s/he use the books in conjunction with other materials.

The secondary social studies curriculum of most school districts does not devote significant time directly to the Caribbean. However, this should not discourage teachers from using these materials. There are many opportunities to address the region within the scope and sequence of traditional social studies and language arts curricula.

The major ways of integrating the Caribbean are through the study of (a) United States history, (b) social studies themes, (c) current events, and (d) language arts. Many of the lessons could be introduced as students are studying the history of the United States or the Western Hemisphere. For example, Unit 3, *The Marcus Garvey Movement*, links the history of the Caribbean and the United States through a study of this historic figure.

The Caribbean can illustrate many required social studies themes and issues. For example, Unit 5, *In the Country*, can be used in studies of economic development; Units 5 and 7 address women's role in the economy and society; and Units 4 and 6 provide examples of the relationship between art/ literature and social change.

This collection also lends itself to cross-disciplinary studies, such as social studies and music, or English and art. Unit 6, *From Rasta to Reggae*, uses popular music as a window on Jamaican social history. In Unit 1, *Anansi, Brer Rabbit, and the Folk Tradition*, students examine connections between the African, Jamaican, and Afro-American folk traditions, and they are encouraged to write and illustrate their own folk tales.

Through some of the suggested activities students can share elements of the history and culture of Jamaica with the rest of the school. For Unit 2, *Our Jamaican Heritage*, students can create for the school halls or main office. After studying Unit 3, on Marcus Garvey, students could create a play about his life to be presented at school assemblies. As a wrap-up activity, students could work in small groups to develop presentations on one or more of the topics studied. A memo could then be circulated to other social studies and language arts teachers offering these presentations during specified class periods. Time should be allowed during each of these presentation for questions and answers. This discussion will motivate the presenting group to do more research and perhaps to learn about additional countries in the Caribbean.

The present series of books is a first edition and will be revised based on feedback received. The editors would be pleased to hear from instructors and students who have used the materials. We want to know how the materials are being used, which parts have proved most effective in the classroom and which need improvement.

Acknowledgements

DEVELOPING THIS RESOURCE involved many people, and was largely a labor of love. We are grateful to Honor Ford-Smith, former artistic director of the Sistren Theater Collective in Kingston, Jamaica, for her advice throughout the project. Members of the Council of Caribbean Organizations in the Baltimore/Washington area provided a useful critical review of the materials. Teacher reviews were carried out by Judy Aaronson of the District of Columbia Public Schools and Virginia Wilkinson of Abington Friends School in Jenkintown, Pennsylvania.

We wish to thank the Center for Educational Design and Communication, a project of the Religious of the Sacred Heart, for their excellent work on production. Melanie Guste, RSCJ, created the design which brought the materials alive. Kathy Davin, a teacher at the District of Columbia's Oyster Bilingual School, assisted with research, editing and proofreading. Laura Margosian and Terry Morgan typed much of the original manuscript. We thank Sally Harriston, a teacher at Wilson High School in Washington, DC, for her help in administering the project.

The D.C. Community Humanities Council, an affiliate of the National Endowment for the Humanities, provided the initial grant for the Caribbean Connections series. Other support came from the CarEth Foundation, the Anita L. Mishler Education Fund, and the Women's Division, Board of Global Ministries, United Methodist Church.

THE PUBLISHERS would like to thank the following for their permission to use copyrighted material:

The author for "Anansi and Brer Goat" by P. Hyacinth Galloway, Traditions, 1986; University of California Press for "The President Wants No More of Anansi" from The Drum and the Hoe: Life and Lore of the Haitian People by Harold Courlander, 1960; Caribbean Review, Inc., Florida International University, for "Anansi and the Magic Calabash" by Althea V. Prince; the author for "The Magic Hoe" from The Hat-Shaking Dance and Other Ashanti Tales from Ghana by Harold Courlander, Harcourt Brace Jovanovich, 1957; University of Georgia Press for "The Magic Hoe" from Drums and Shadows: Survival Studies Among the Georgia Coastal Negroes edited by the Georgia Writers' Project, 1940; Hope McKay Virtue for "My Green Hills of Jamaica" from My Green Hills of Jamaica by Claude McKay, Heinemann, 1979; the author for "African Roots of My Jamaican Heritage" from The Sun and the Drum: African Roots in Jamaican Folk Tradition by Leonard Barrett, Heinemann, 1976; Africa World Press for "Remembering Marcus Garvey" from Marcus Garvey's Footsoldiers of the Universal Negro Improvement Association by Jeannette Smith-Irvin, 1987; the author and Grove Weidenfeld for "Burying Miss 'Mando" from The Harder They Come by Michael Thelwell, 1980; the author and Sister Vision: Black Women and Women of Colour Press for "Miss Lou" and "Miss Tiny" from Blaze A Fire: Significant Contributions of Caribbean Women by Nesha Z. Haniff, 1988; the author for "Colonization in Reverse," "Back to Africa," and "Dutty Tough," by Louise Bennett; the author for "Pressure Drop" by Oku Onuora; Sistren Theater Collective for "Tribute to Gloria Who Overcame Death."

Every effort has been made to locate copyright holders for the granting of permission. The editors would be glad to hear from anyone who has been inadvertently overlooked in order to make the necessary changes at the first opportunity.

▼ GRAPHICS CREDITS

Cover design by Betty Shearman, RSCJ and Melanie Guste, RSCJ

pp.10-11 Ecumenical Program on Central America and the Caribbean

p.15 (left) Courtesy of the Caribbean Cultural Center, New York City

p.15 (right) Jamaica Information Service

p.16 Jamaica Information Service

p.17 (top) Jamaica Information Service

p.17 (bottom) Jamaica *Daily Gleaner*

p.18 (top) Jamaica Information Service

p.18 (bottom) Inter-American Development Bank

p.19 Courtesy of the Embassy of Jamaica, Washington, DC

p.20 Workers Party of Jamaica

p.21 Jim Richter

pp.25-29 Courtesy of P. Hyacinth Galloway

p.37 Albert Huie, from *Jamaica Journal*

p.39 Michelle Gibbs

p.47 *Jamaica Journal*

p.48 Jamaica Information Service

p.49 *Jamaica Journal*

pp.50-51 Courtesy of Theresa Moore

p.64 Michelle Gibbs

p.67 Vernal Reuben, from *Jamaica Journal*

p.68 Workers Party of Jamaica

pp.71-73 Katherine Rawson

p.76 Michelle Gibbs

p.81 *Everybody's Magazine*

p.90 Sistren Theater Collective

p.93 Juan C. Urquiola, from *Caribbean Review*

p.98 Vernal Reuben, from *Jamaica Journal*

p.101 Sistren Theater Collective

BERMUDA
Hamilton
Col. U.K.
Crown Colony
Pop. 72,000

BAHAMAS
Nassau
Col. U.K.
Ind. 1973
Pop. 241,000

CUBA
Havana
Col. Spain
Ind. 1898
Pop. 9.8 million

CAYMAN ISLANDS
Georgetown
Col. U.K.
Crown Colony
Pop. 20,000

JAMAICA
Kingston
Col. U.K.
Ind. 1962
Pop. 2.2 million

BELIZE
Belmopan
Col. U.K.
Ind. 1981
Pop. 152,000

**NETHERLANDS
ANTILLES**
1. Curaçao
2. Aruba
3. Bonaire
4. St. Maarten
5. Saba
6. St. Eustatius
Willemstad
Col. Holland
Self-governing
   colony
Pop. 260,000

FRENCH GUIANA
Cayenne
Col. France
French overseas
   department
Pop. 77,000

SURINAME
Paramaribo
Col. Holland
Ind. 1975
Pop. 376,000

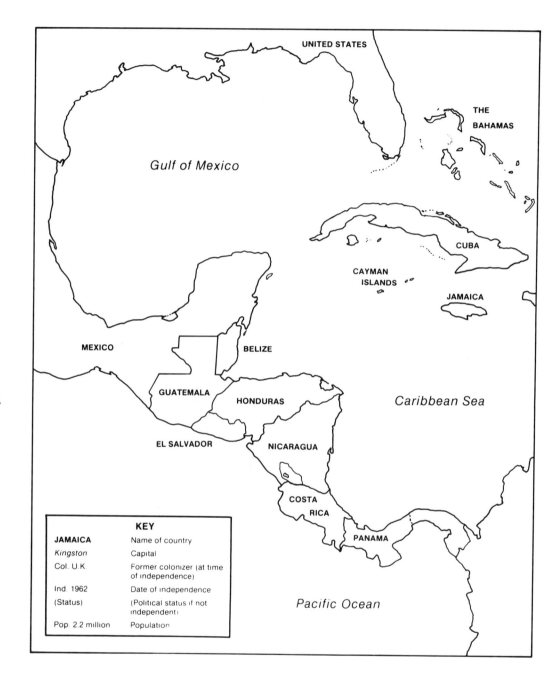

KEY

JAMAICA	Name of country
Kingston	Capital
Col. U.K.	Former colonizer (at time of independence)
Ind. 1962	Date of independence
(Status)	(Political status if not independent)
Pop. 2.2 million	Population

GUYANA
Georgetown
Col. U.K.
Ind. 1966
Pop. 700,000

**TRINIDAD
AND TOBAGO**
Port-of-Spain
Col. U.K.
Ind. 1962
Pop. 1.1 million

GRENADA
St. George's
Col. U.K.
Ind. 1974
Pop. 110,000

BARBADOS
Bridgetown
Col. U.K.
Ind. 1966
Pop. 256,000

**ST. VINCENT &
THE GRENADINES**
Kingstown
Col. U.K.
Ind. 1979
Pop. 123,000

TURKS & CAICOS
Grand Turk
Col. U.K.
Crown Colony
Pop. 8,000

HAITI
Port-au-Prince
Col. France
Ind. 1804
Pop. 5.2 million

DOMINICAN REPUBLIC
Santo Domingo
Col. Spain
Ind. 1844
Pop. 6.3 million

PUERTO RICO
San Juan
Col. Spain/U.S.
U.S. possession
Pop. 3.2 million

BRITISH VIRGIN IS.
Road Town
Col. U.K.
British dependency
Pop. 13,000

U.S. VIRGIN IS.
1. St. Thomas
2. St. Croix
3. St. John
Charlotte Amalie
Col. U.S.
U.S. territory
Pop. 103,000

ANGUILLA
The Valley
Col. U.K.
British dependency
Pop. 7,000

ANTIGUA & BARBUDA
St. John
Col. U.K.
Ind. 1981
Pop. 77,000

ST. KITTS/NEVIS
Basseterre
Col. U.K.
Ind. 1983
Pop. 45,000

The Caribbean

ST. LUCIA
Castries
Col. U.K.
Ind. 1979
Pop. 119,000

MARTINIQUE
Fort-de-France
Col. France
French overseas department
Pop. 303,000

DOMINICA
Roseau
Col. U.K.
Ind. 1978
Pop. 74,000

GUADELOUPE
Basseterre
Col. France
French overseas department
Pop. 328,000

MONTSERRAT
Plymouth
Col. U.K.
Crown Colony
Pop. 12,000

Map Exercises

ACTIVITY 1: FIND THESE COUNTRIES

Instructor: For this exercise, white-out the names of the following countries on the master map. Make a photocopy of the altered map for each student. Break the class into small groups. The groups will use the clues to fill in the names of the missing countries on their maps. They will think of another fact they know about each country and write it in the space provided. (If they do not know, encourage them to guess.) Afterwards, go over each set of clues with the class, asking a student to point out the correct country on a large wall map.

1. **The Dominican Republic** is a Spanish-speaking country. It shares the island of Hispaniola with Haiti.
Something else we know about the Dominican Republic:_____

_____

2. **Barbados** is an English-speaking country. It is the easternmost island in the Caribbean Sea.
Something else we know about Barbados: _____

_____

3. **Trinidad and Tobago** is a twin-island state. It is off the coast of Venezuela at the southern tip of the Caribbean archipelago.
Something else we know about Trinidad and Tobago:_____

_____

4. **Guyana** is an English-speaking country on the South American mainland. It shares a border with Venezuela.
Something else we know about Guyana: _____

_____

5. **Belize** is an English-speaking country located in Central America. It shares borders with Guatemala and Mexico.
Something else we know about Belize: _____

_____

6. **Dominica** is an English-speaking country. It is located between the French territories of Guadeloupe and Martinique.
Something else we know about Dominica: _____

_____

7. **Curaçao** is a Dutch colony. It is off the coast of Venezuela between Aruba and Bonaire.
Something else we know about Curaçao: _____

_____

ACTIVITY 2: WHO AM I?

Instructor: Photocopy the worksheet below for each student. Students will retain their maps from the preceding activity. Break the class into small groups. Each group will fill in the country names on the worksheet and add their own "clues." Afterwards, go over each set of clues with the class, asking a student to point out the correct country on a large wall map.

1. I am an archipelago of many small islands.
I am close to Florida.
My capital is Nassau.

I *am* _____

Our own clue: _____

2. I am south of St. Vincent.
I produce nutmeg.
The United States invaded me in 1983.

I *am* _____

Our own clue: _____

3. I am one of three Spanish-speaking Caribbean nations.
I am near the U.S. Virgin Islands.
I am a United States "Commonwealth."

I *am* _____

Our own clue: _____

4. I am the largest island in the Caribbean.
My capital is Havana.
I produce sugar.

I *am* _____

Our own clue: _____

5. I was colonized by France.
I had a successful slave revolution in 1795.
I share an island with the Dominican Republic.

I *am* _____

Our own clue: _____

6. I am an island south of Cuba.
I produce bauxite.
I am the birthplace of reggae music.

I *am* _____

Our own clue: _____

Jamaica at a Glance

Official name: Jamaica

Political status: Independent (gained independence from Britain in 1962). Member of the British Commonwealth and of the Caribbean Community (CARICOM).

Form of government: A legislature, called Parliament, is made up of a House of Representatives, a Senate, and the Queen of England. The leader of the majority party in the House of Representatives is appointed Prime Minister and heads the government. The Queen is titular head of state and is represented in Jamaica by a Governor-General. The Constitution provides for the Prime Minister to serve for up to five years before calling a general election.

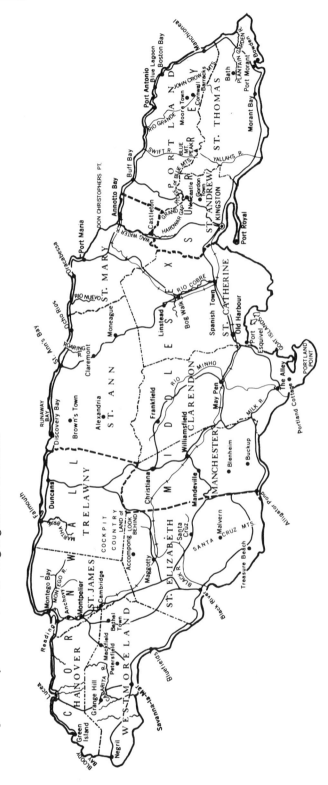

Area: 4,411 square miles. Third largest of the Caribbean islands.

Population: 2.4 million (1982)

Capital: Kingston

Second largest city: Montego Bay

Language: English. Most people also speak an English-based Creole language known as patois.

Currency: Jamaican dollar

A Brief History of Jamaica

Long before the Europeans arrived, Jamaica was a homeland of the Arawak people. Originally from South America, the Arawaks began migrating north into the Caribbean around 500 B.C. They established their main settlements on the islands today known as the Bahamas, Hispaniola, Cuba, Jamaica and Puerto Rico. The Arawaks called Jamaica "Xaymaca," meaning "land of wood and water."

The Arawaks were a peaceful people who lived by farming,

An Arawak cemí

hunting and fishing. Corn and cassava were their most important crops. They lived in permanent villages called *yucayeques*, each governed by a *cacique* or chief. They worshipped various gods, and carved figures from stone, clay, wood or gold—called *cemís*—to drive away evil spirits and ensure a good harvest.

Christopher Columbus landed on Jamaica during his second voyage, in 1494, and claimed the island for Spain. The Spanish settlers forced the Arawaks to work on farms and ranches and in unproductive gold mines. Despite frequent Arawak rebellions, overwork, abuse and disease eventually killed off the entire Arawak population.

To replace the Arawaks' labor, the Spanish turned to Africa. The first African slaves arrived in Jamaica in 1517.

In 1655 Britain sent out an invasion force which seized Jamaica from Spain. The British takeover led to a huge expansion of slavery in Jamaica. British colonists set up plantations to supply raw sugar to Britain, each worked by hundreds of slaves. Many plantation owners lived in England, and the overseers they left to run their estates often abused the slaves cruelly.

But the Africans in Jamaica outnumbered the Europeans by a ratio of ten to one. Many came from the Akan peoples of West Africa, who were skilled warriors. Resistance to slavery was continuous and often violent; Jamaica had more slave revolts than any other Caribbean colony. In 1760 a man named Tackey led an uprising of more than 1,000 slaves. But the colonial authorities crushed the rebellion, and Tackey was killed.

Slaves also resisted by running away. Jamaica's rugged mountains and gullies made it possible for escaped slaves to set up hidden villages beyond reach of the planters. The rebels, called "maroons," waged two guerrilla wars against the British. A maroon leader named

Nanny of the Maroons

Nanny was the most courageous of all in refusing to yield to the slave owners. Today she is a national heroine of Jamaica.

Religious movements played an important role in the slaves' resistance. *Myalism* was based on the idea that misfortunes were the result of sorcery, and that certain rituals could protect against harm. Based on African beliefs, myalism later blended with elements of the Baptist religion. Myalists and "Native Baptists" became a driving force in Jamaicans' resistance against European control.

In 1831 Sam Sharpe, a Native Baptist lay preacher and myalist, led a huge slave revolt. The uprising was one factor which pushed the British finally to end slavery. Emancipation was declared in 1834, but the slaves were not actually freed. Instead, they were required to continue working on the plantations for another four years, a period known as "apprenticeship." Full freedom was granted in 1838.

After Emancipation: Resistance Continues

The Africans in Jamaica came from societies rich in art, music and folklore. Crafts such as woodcarving, which required special materials, could not continue on the plantations. But many religious and social customs, as well as storytelling, music and dance, survived. They became part of the heritage of Africans in the Americas. (*Anansi, Brer Rabbit and the Folk Tradition*)

After emancipation, the colonial authorities wanted the former slaves to continue working on the plantations for low wages. They knew that African culture and religion helped unify the ex-slaves and encourage resistance, so they attempted to suppress them. Drumming, which had been associated with slave revolts,

was banned. Myalism was driven underground through persecution.

The missionary churches played an important role. The Roman Catholic Church and the Anglican Church (the Church of England) had the longest history on the island. But after emancipation, Baptist, Methodist, and Moravian missionaries took the lead in educating and assisting the former slaves. Missionaries purchased land for "free villages" away from the plantations. They also set up the first schools for Afro-Jamaicans.

In this way the churches helped the former slaves to become economically independent. At the same time, through their teachings, they pressured Afro-Jamaicans to abandon African cultural traditions and to accept a subservient social role.

Jamaicans did adopt many aspects of British culture, and these became an important part of the Jamaican identity. But African-influenced traditions also continued as an unofficial, often suppressed, but powerful cultural force. (*Our Jamaican Heritage*) In 1860-1861 Baptist and Moravian missionaries attempted to lead a revival of Christian religious fervor. But the movement quickly became Africanized, providing a channel through which myalism surged forth once again. This blending of African and Christian religion produced "Revivalism," a complex of religious cults which remain strong in Jamaica.

After emancipation, many of the planters and merchants returned to England. Some sold

their land to U.S. or British companies; others simply abandoned their estates. Groups of former slaves pooled their savings and bought land together, or squatted on abandoned land. In this way hundreds of small farms and free villages were created.

The years following emancipation were desperately hard for these independent farmers. The Europeans who remained in the colony still controlled the government and most of the best land. They used unfair laws, evictions and taxes to hinder the ex-slaves from acquiring land of their own. Rather than pay fair wages for plantation work, the planters brought in contract laborers from India, China and Africa as a new source of cheap labor.

In 1865, the arrest of a Black

Paul Bogle

farmer for "trespassing" on farmland set off a violent riot in the eastern town of Morant Bay.

Led by Paul Bogle and George William Gordon, the uprising was an explosion of pent-up anger and frustration. The response of the colonial authorities was brutal: troops killed 439 people and burned 1,000 homes. Bogle and Gordon were arrested and hanged. Today, Jamaicans recognize them as national heroes for their brave attempt to win justice for the poor.

Over time, a small middle class—including teachers, pastors, journalists and lawyers—gained a voice in the island's affairs. But the working-class majority, some 90 percent of the population, was still excluded. Many suffered severe poverty, farming small hilly plots or working on sugar or banana plantations for a few cents a day.

The Impact of Marcus Garvey

Into this situation stepped a legendary leader, Marcus Garvey. Born in Jamaica in 1887, he formed a mass movement of Black people which had members throughout the Caribbean, in the United States, and in other parts of the world.

Garvey spoke out forcefully against racism and colonialism. He demanded "Africa for the Africans, at home and abroad." He urged people of African descent to unite as one nation and to look to Africa, particularly Ethiopia, as their rightful home. (*The Marcus Garvey Movement*)

Garvey's vision influenced

almost all the Black political movements which followed, in both Jamaica and the United States. One of these was Rastafarianism, which had religious roots in the Ethiopianist movement and the Jamaican Afro-Christian tradition. Garvey is reported to have said, "Look to Africa, where a Black King will be crowned, for the day of deliverance is near." When King Ras Tafari of Ethiopia was crowned Emperor Haile Selassie in 1930, many Jamaicans saw Garvey's words as prophecy. A growing cult of followers, called Rastafarians, proclaimed Selassie to be the living God. "Repatriation" to Africa became a focal aim of the movement.

During the 1930s, a depression led to even greater unem-

banana workers, sugar workers, dock workers and unemployed people went on strike, shutting down the city of Kingston for two days.

Independent Jamaica

The strikes were a turning point. The workers did not win all their demands, but they

Sir Alexander Bustamante

Front page of the Jamaica Daily Gleaner reports the outbreak of strikes in 1938.

ployment and hunger on the island. Desperate for change, Jamaican workers organized under the leadership of several former Garveyites, demanding higher wages and access to land. In 1938 thousands of

gained the important right to join trade unions. Alexander Bustamante, who had played a leading role in the strikes, formed the Bustamante Industrial Trade Union, a powerful labor organization. He and his cousin Norman Manley together founded the People's National Party (PNP), which brought pressure on the British government to move Jamaica toward self-government.

Norman Washington Manley

In 1944, for the first time in Jamaica's history, a new constitution granted all adults the right to vote. The year before, Bustamante had parted ways from Manley and formed the Jamaica Labor Party. Now, Jamaican working people voting for the first time threw their support behind the two parties.

In 1962, Jamaica and Trinidad became the first of Britain's Caribbean colonies to gain independence. Jamaicans celebrated as their green, yellow and black flag was raised. Colonialism was behind them; Jamaica was now a sovereign nation.

Although it joined the British Commonwealth, Jamaica was no longer bound exclusively to England as the "mother country." It could establish trade and diplomatic ties with any country. Jamaica gained a seat in regional and international organizations, including the United Nations, the Organization of American States, and the Caribbean Community (CARICOM).

The island's government and its legal system remained based on the British model. The Queen of England became the symbolic head of state, represented in Jamaica by a Governor-General. A Parliament, or legislature, was made up of elected and appointed members, with the leader of the majority party as the Prime Minister, or head of the government.

Independence brought significant changes in some aspects of national life. The educational system expanded, enabling more Jamaicans to attend high school and college. Jamaicans also began to look at ways to make education, long based on British models, more relevant to Jamaican life. And for the first time, Jamaica acquired its own university—the University of the West Indies, where students from all over the Caribbean would come to be educated.

Perhaps the most significant change, however, was in the ways Jamaicans thought about themselves and their country. Literature and the arts became important means of defining a national identity. The pioneers of Jamaican literature—Claude

Students at the College of Arts, Science and Technology in Kingston, Jamaica. Access to higher education expanded after independence.

McKay, Herbert DeLisser and Tom Redcam—had written about Jamaican life in the early twentieth century. During the 1950s and 1960s, new authors emerged to interpret the Jamaican experience. Louise Bennett's poetry celebrated the lives and language of ordinary working people. (*Louise Bennett, National Poetess of Jamaica*) Novelists Roger Mais, John Hearne, Victor Reid, and Andrew Salkey, playwright Trevor Rhone, and other authors won recognition for Jamaica's literature. The Jamaica National Dance Theater Company, founded by artist Rex Nettleford, led the way in a creative flowering of the dramatic arts.

The start of bauxite mining in 1952 dramatically changed the Jamaican economy.

In other areas, however, independence brought few changes. The economy was still largely foreign-controlled. Bauxite, the material from which aluminum is made, was discovered in Jamaica in 1942. In the 1950s two North American firms, Reynolds of the U.S. and Alcan

of Canada, began mining and exporting Jamaican bauxite. Bauxite became the island's most important export.

At the same time, Jamaica, like other Caribbean countries, offered incentives to foreign firms to invest in the island's economy. The island attracted mining, tourism, manufacturing, financial, transportation and communications industries, almost all of them based in the United States, Canada or Britain.

The rapidly growing tourist industry likewise found its main market in North America. Eighty-five percent of visitors to Jamaica came from the United States and Canada.

Some Jamaicans benefitted from their partnership with these foreign firms, and the middle class expanded. Most Jamaicans, however, still lived and worked in the rural areas as poorly-paid agricultural workers or struggling small farmers. (*In the Country*) For many people, the years following independence brought only deeper poverty and unemployment.

One solution was emigration. Thousands of Jamaicans migrated to England, prompting

poet Louise Bennett to joke about Jamaicans "colonizing England in reverse." Later, the exodus turned toward the United States and Canada.

Rural people also migrated to the capital, Kingston, swelling the crowded urban shantytowns. Out of this experience of ghetto life came a new music that was uniquely Jamaican, although it would become popular throughout the world. Reggae was based partly on Rastafarian styles of singing and drumming. Leading reggae artists, like Bob Marley and the Wailers, were Rastafarians. Their songs spoke powerfully of suffering in Jamaica and of a promised land in Africa. (*From Rasta to Reggae*)

Better Must Come?

Michael Manley, Norman Manley's son, led the government from 1972 to 1980. Under the campaign slogan "Better Must Come," he introduced many programs benefiting the poor. These included a jobs program, a literacy campaign, a minimum wage law, and land reform. Manley's government also required the foreign-owned aluminum companies to give Jamaica a fair price for the bauxite they mined from the island.

Manley was reelected in 1976, but his government faced severe problems. To earn foreign exchange, Jamaica sold bauxite, sugar and bananas to the industrialized countries. Prices for these were falling on the world market, meaning less income for Jamaica. At the same time, Jamaica had to import food, machinery and other goods at prices which were rising. The sharp increase in the price of imported oil in 1973 hurt Jamaica and many other developing countries.

Many U.S. officials and Jamaican business leaders opposed the Manley government's foreign policy positions, and they objected to his demands on the bauxite companies. As a result, the U.S. government and international banks sharply cut their loans and aid to Jamaica.

By the late 1970s, Jamaica was nearly bankrupt. Manley's government signed an agreement with the International Monetary Fund (IMF), a lending agency, for a large loan. As a condition for the loan, IMF officials would dictate the economic policies Jamaica should follow.

Under the IMF plan, the Jamaican government had to cut its spending on social programs such as jobs, literacy and health care. It had to remove most subsidies and price controls, allowing the costs of food and other necessities to rise. Thousands of public employees were fired, and new taxes imposed.

These hardships shattered confidence in Manley's government. His People's National Party lost in the 1980 election, and Edward Seaga of the Jamaica Labor Party became the new prime minister.

Unlike Manley, Seaga enjoyed good relations with U.S. officials and international bankers. But

he faced the same economic dilemma. Falling demand for bauxite continued to lower Jamaica's earnings from its most important export. Officials hoped for new investment by foreign manufacturing firms, but only a few firms invested.

Jamaican women protest rising prices in 1980.

Garment factories owned by U.S. and Asian companies provided jobs for some 20,000 Jamaican women, but at very low wages. Only tourism brought healthy financial returns.

In exchange for loans from the IMF and the World Bank, Seaga's government laid off still more workers. Prices for food skyrocketed, and schools, clinics and public transportation deteriorated from neglect. In 1989, Jamaicans voted Seaga out in a landslide, and Manley became prime minister once again.

While tourists at the island's posh resorts buy t-shirts that

proclaim "Jamaica - No Problem," the reality for many Jamaicans is different. For many, life has become a daily battle to cope with overcrowded buses, hospitals without medicines, and schools without books, paper or chalk.

Many Jamaicans now doubt that any leader or political party alone can solve the country's problems. Increasingly, they are looking for solutions on their own, organizing cultural groups, job-training programs, health clinics and more. Some, like the Sistren Theater Collective, work to raise the public's awareness of problems facing the poor. (*Women's Theater in Jamaica*) These efforts are still small-scale. But they offer hope that in the future, as so often in the past, the resistant spirit of the Jamaican people will be the motor force for change.

Further Reading on Jamaican History

Clinton V. Black, *History of Jamaica* (Collins, 1965).

Philip D. Curtin, *Two Jamaicas: The Role of Ideas in a Tropical Colony 1830-1865* (Negro Univ. Press, 1972).

Douglas Hall, *Free Jamaica 1838-1865: An Economic History* (Caribbean Universities Press, 1969).

Michael Kaufman, *Jamaica Under Manley: Dilemmas of Socialism and Democracy* (Zed Books, 1985).

Michael Manley, *The Politics of Change: A Jamaican Testament* (Deutsch, 1974).

Orlando Patterson, *The Sociology of Slavery* (Sangster's Book Stores, 1967).

Carey Robinson, *The Fighting Maroons of Jamaica* (Sangster's Book Stores, 1969).

Olive Senior, *A-Z of Jamaican Heritage* (Heinemann/The Gleaner Co., 1983).

Evelyne H. and John D. Stephens, *Democratic Socialism in Jamaica* (Princeton Univ. Press, 1986).

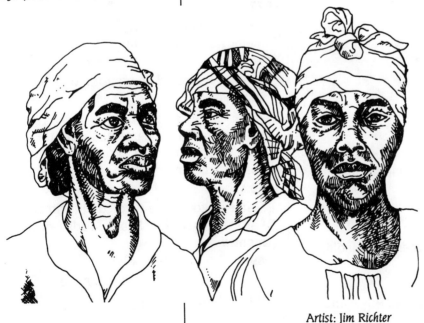

Artist: Jim Richter

Important Dates in Jamaican History

pre-1492
Jamaica is a homeland of the Arawaks, a native people originally from South America. They call the island "Xaymaca."

1494
Columbus lands on his second voyage and claims the island for Spain.

1509-1655
Spanish colonial rule. Arawaks killed off by forced labor, massacres and disease.

1517
First African slaves arrive.

1655
Jamaica becomes a British colony with large-scale sugar production.

1655-1670
Headquarters for British buccaneers.

1734-1738
First Maroon War, ended by treaty between the Maroons and the British.

1760
Slave revolt led by Tackey.

1795-1796
Second Maroon War.

1807
Britain ends slave trade.

1831-1832
Slave revolt led by Sam Sharpe.

1834
Emancipation proclamation. Slaves begin four-year "apprenticeship" on the plantations.

1838
Slaves fully freed.

1845-1917
Importation of contract laborers from India, China, Africa and Europe.

1865
Morant Bay rebellion led by Paul Bogle and George William Gordon.

1928-1935
Marcus Garvey organizing in Jamaica.

1938
Riots of workers and the unemployed. Alexander Bustamante and Norman Manley form the People's National Party.

1943
Bustamante forms the Jamaica Labor Party.

1944
First election under universal adult suffrage.

1948
University College of the West Indies established.

1952
U.S. and Canadian companies begin exporting Jamaican bauxite.

1959
Jamaica receives internal self-government in preparation for independence.

1962
Jamaica becomes independent.

1972
People's National Party elected. Michael Manley becomes prime minister.

1976
Manley reelected on platform of "democratic socialism."

1977
Manley signs loan agreement with the International Monetary Fund. Stringent economic austerity begins.

1980
Manley's government voted out. Jamaica Labor Party under Edward Seaga heads new government.

1989
Seaga's government voted out. People's National Party under Michael Manley takes office again.

UNIT ONE: Anansi, Brer Rabbit and the Folk Tradition
TEACHER GUIDE

▶ **OBJECTIVES**

Students will:

1. Enjoy Anansi stories, an important part of the Jamaican folk tradition

2. Identify shared elements in the folktales of African-American, African and Afro-Caribbean peoples

3. Compare and contrast storytelling and television as transmitters of cultural messages

▶ **QUESTIONS FOR DISCUSSION**

1. What would you have done for entertainment had you lived before radio, TV and movies were invented? What if you lived in a society that did not have books?

2. What are the purposes of storytelling? How do they differ from the purposes of television, radio or movies?

3. Locate Jamaica, Antigua, Haiti, Ghana and Georgia (USA) on a map. Why do their folktales have elements in common?

4. Did Anansi obey the President? Explain. (Haiti story)

5. How would you describe the relationship between Bruh Rabbit and Bruh Wolf? (Georgia story)

6. Compare the two versions of "The Magic Hoe" from West Africa and the United States. Why do you think the story changed as it did?

7. What moral messages can you find in these stories? How do they compare with folktales you know? How are similar messages conveyed in your own culture?

▶ **SUGGESTED ACTIVITIES**

1. [Middle school students] Students can illustrate the stories from Haiti, Antigua, Georgia and Ghana. You may wish to collaborate with an art teacher on this project.

2. [Middle school students] Divide the class into five groups. Give each student a copy of the story his/her group will read. Each group will prepare and perform a skit based on the story assigned them.

After each presentation, the group that performed the skit leads a discussion based on the story. The group should prepare questions in advance. After the presentations, lead a wrap-up discussion on common themes in the stories.

3. Students write their own Anansi stories. Stories may be set in a modern context, but should embody principal themes of the Anansi tradition. When

stories are completed, divide the class into small groups. Each group will select one story to share with the rest of the class. Producing illustrated booklets of students' Anansi stories is a possible follow-up.

4. Ask students to think about the role television plays in their lives. Next, lead a discussion of the differences and similarities between television and storytelling. Questions to consider: What does the audience see and hear? Who decides what the content will be? What kind of moral or social messages are conveyed? What is the role of the audience? What, ultimately, is the goal and purpose? A helpful source for analyzing television's impact is *The Plug-In Drug* by Marie Winn (Viking, 1985).

You may wish to assign written essays based on the discussion.

▶ **RESOURCES**

1. Jamaican educator P. Hyacinth Galloway narrates three Anansi stories on tape: "Brer Anancy and Brer Goat," "Brer Anancy and Bird Cherry Island," and "Brer Anancy and the Chief's Daughter." Each cassette comes with the story text in an illustrated booklet. Available from Traditions, P.O. Box 3827, Hyattsville, MD 20787.

2. Laura Tanna, *Jamaican Folk Tales and Oral Histories* (Institute of Jamaica, 1986). The stories in this book were transcribed from actual performances by Jamaican storytellers (in Jamaican patois). An audio cassette and video (58 and 104 minute versions) are sold separately. Available from Caribbean Books.

3. Velma Pollard, ed., *Anansesem: A Collection of Caribbean Folk Tales, Legends and Poems for Juniors* (Longman Jamaica, 1985). Selections from various Caribbean countries, suitable for younger students.

4. Walter Jekyll, *Jamaica Song and Story* (Dover Pub., 1966). Anansi stories, digging songs, ring tunes and dancing tunes.

5. Andrew Salkey, *Anancy's Score* (Bogle L'Ouverture, 1973). Twenty Anansi stories, mostly in patois.

6. Two collections of African and African-American folktales, including some Anansi stories:

Roger D. Abrahams, ed., *Afro-American Folktales: Stories from Black Traditions in the New World* (Pantheon Books/Random House, 1985).

Harold Courlander, *A Treasury of African Folklore* (Crown Publishing, 1975).

INTRODUCTION
Anansi, Brer Rabbit and the Folk Tradition

Before radio, television and movies were invented, people in many parts of the world created their own entertainment. Storytelling was especially popular. Telling folk tales and histories served not only as amusement, but also as a way of remembering and passing on ideas in an age when most people could not read or write.

In West Africa, storytelling was a richly developed art. Villagers would gather around a fire at night to hear one of their neighbors—perhaps an old woman or man—tell favorite tales. The Ashanti people, who live in Ghana today, often told stories about a spider named Anansi. Many of the Africans brought to Jamaica were Ashanti, and they brought the Anansi folk tales with them. Anansi stories are told in Jamaica and throughout the Caribbean.

Although supposedly a spider, Anansi has human qualities. He is a "trickster," a small, weak figure who gets his way through intelligence and cunning. Anansi's goal is to live well—especially to eat well—while working as little as possible. He often fools stronger characters such as Tiger, Monkey and Dog, or sometimes the King or President. But when Anansi goes too far with greed or selfishness, he is punished, as in "Anansi and the Magic Calabash." Some Anansi stories explain how or why something came about, as in "Anansi and Brer Goat."

The same trickster figure came to the United States with the Africans brought to the U.S. colonies. In the African-American folk tradition, the character is usually a rabbit instead of a spider. Brer Rabbit has many of the same qualities as Anansi—a small, weak figure who outwits bigger and stronger opponents.

Brer Rabbit stories are especially common in the coastal areas of Georgia and South Carolina. There, isolated Black communities maintained aspects of their African heritage after these traditions had faded elsewhere. The similarity between "The Magic Hoe" as told in Georgia, U.S.A., and Ghana, West Africa, shows the shared roots of the African, African-American and Afro-Caribbean folk traditions.

In addition to the Anansi tales, Jamaican folklore includes other types of "old-time" stories and word games. These include duppy stories (ghost stories), historical narratives, "Big Boy" stories, riddles, rhymes and songs.

Although supposedly a spider, Anansi has human qualities.

READING
Anansi and Brer Goat

A FOLK TALE FROM JAMAICA

Once upon a time, there was a spider by the name of Anansi. In those days, everyone was called "Brer," which is short for "Brother," so Anansi was called "Brer Anansi," and the goat was called "Brer Goat."

One day when Brer Anansi was without a job, he heard that a man wanted a watchman to work in his banana field. Anansi had never worked as a watchman, but he saw where he might be able to get some food for himself and his family if he took this job. So Anansi applied for the job. When he met the owner of the field, Mr. Mann, Mr. Mann said to him, "You are so small, Anansi; are you sure you can do this job?"

"Yes, said Anansi, "I will do a good job."

Mr. Mann hired Brer Anansi as the watchman for his field of bananas, but Mr. Mann noticed that from the day he hired Anansi, the bananas began to disappear.

Mr. Mann went back to Anansi and said, "Brer Anansi, you are not doing a good job. Someone is stealing my bananas!"

"I don't know how that could happen," said Anansi. "I watch the field every night and I don't see anyone."

"Anansi," said Mr. Mann, "You have to do better than this. I can't afford to lose any more bananas."

"All right, Mr. Mann," said Anansi. "I am going to do better!"

With this, Mr. Mann went away. However, he did not trust Anansi. He had become suspicious of him, so he decided to set a trap and see if he could

Mr. Mann got some tar and painted the trunk of the banana tree.

catch the thief.

One day when Anansi was absent, Mr. Mann got some tar and painted the trunk of the banana tree that had the loveliest bunch of bananas. He felt sure that the thief would want to take that particular bunch of bananas. If he tried, he would get stuck.

That night, Mr. Mann hid in the field and waited to see what would happen. As usual, Anansi arrived for work, and as he was used to doing, he walked around the field looking for the best bunch of bananas. As he walked, he saw something which resembled a man with arms stretched out. This was really the banana tree that Mr. Mann had painted. In the moonlight, the wet tar gave off a shiny glow, and the tree trunk looked like a man while the big leaves⁰ looked like the man's arms waving in the air.

Anansi was afraid, but he drew himself up to his full height, and in his deepest voice he shouted, "Hey you! What are you doing in Mr. Mann's field?

There was no answer.

Anansi called again: "Hey! I'm talking to you. What are you doing here?" There was still no answer.

Anansi became annoyed. "I am giving you one more chance," he said, "and then you are going to be sorry."

Still there was no answer. Anansi stepped back, made a fist and hit the man with a heavy right punch. To Anansi's surprise, his hand stuck!

"Let go of my hand!" shrieked Anansi. But his hand stuck fast.

"I say, LET GO! LET GO!"

There was no answer.

"All right," said Anansi, "you are going to get another punch with my left hand."

As Anansi said this, he made a big fist with his left hand and his the "man" again. This time, what do you think happened? The left hand stuck!

"Oh, you want to play," said Anansi. "I am not playing with you! Let go my hands!" Anansi twisted and turned, but there was no answer.

"All right," said Anansi. "This time you've asked for it." Anansi lifted his right foot and kicked the "man." What do you think

happened? His right foot stuck.

Anansi was furious and frustrated. He had one foot free, but he was still fighting.

"I am going to count to three," said Anansi, "and if you have not released me, I am coming at you with my left foot."

Still no answer. Anansi lifted his left foot and kicked the "man," and the left foot stuck.

Poor Anansi! His two hands and two feet were all stuck to the tree!

Brer Anansi knew he was in trouble, but he could do nothing. He thought and thought. Suddenly, he heard a sound, and out of the bushes came Brer Goat.

"Brer Goat," cried Anansi, "I

"I am giving you one more chance!" Anansi cried.

am so glad to see you. Please help me."

"Brer Anansi," said Brer Goat, "why are you up there? I shall certainly help you."

"I am in a little trouble," said Anansi. "If you could go behind this tree and butt it with your head, you could push me off. I am stuck."

Goats are so stupid! They do not think. Brer Goat just took Anansi at his word and went behind the tree. He backed away a little as goats do when they are getting ready to hit something, then he bent his head and rushed at the tree. He hit the tree with such force that Brer Anansi was pushed off and landed safely on his back.

In the meantime, what do you think happened to Brer Goat? He got stuck.

Mr. Mann, who was hiding some distance away, heard all the noise and thought he had surely caught Anansi this time. He came running to the spot, only to find Brer Goat stuck to the tree.

"Brer Goat," said Mr. Mann in astonishment. "Is it really you who has been stealing my bananas all this time? I am shocked!"

Brer Goat realized that he had fallen into a trap. "No, Mr. Mann," he said, "it is Brer—" As he started to say "Brer Anansi," Brer Anansi hit him in his head. This staggered Brer Goat so he could not finish the sentence. As soon as he recovered, Brer Goat started to explain again: "Is Brer—" and again Anansi poked him, this time in his side so that the breath rushed out of Brer Goat and he could not finish his sentence. Brer Goat tried a third time: "Mr. Mann, it is not me. It is Brer —" and again

"I *am in a little trouble*," said Anansi.

Anansi poked him in his side. Anansi poked him so hard that Brer Goat fell of the tree.

Brer Goat jumped up quickly and decided to get away as fast as he could. As he began to run, he still tried to explain, but all that could come out of his mouth was "Brer! Brer! Brer!"

And from that day until now, all that a goat can say is "Brer-a-a! Bra-a-a! Bra-a-a!"

Jack Mandora me no choose none![0]

–Reprinted from: P. Hyacinth Galloway, "Anancy and Brer Goat" (Traditions, 1986).

Vocabulary

big leaves: bananas grow on a low tree with large, broad leaves

Jack Mandora me no choose none: traditional ending to Anansi stories. Its meaning is obscure.

* * * *

READING

The President Wants No More of Anansi

A FOLK TALE FROM HAITI

Anansi and all his smart ways irritated the President so much that the President told him one day: "Anansi, I'm tired of your foolishness. Don't you ever let me see your face again." So Anansi went away from the palace. And a few days later he saw the President coming down the street, so he quickly stuck his head into the open door of a limekiln.⁰

Everyone on the street took off their hats when the President passed. When he came to the limekiln, he saw Anansi's behind sticking out. He became angry and said, "Qui bounda ca qui pas salue mwe?" (Whose behind is it that doesn't salute me?) Anansi took his head out of the limekiln and said, "C'est bounda 'Nansi qui pas salue ou." (It's Anansi's behind which didn't salute you.)

The President said angrily, "Anansi, you don't respect me." Anansi said: "President, I was just doing what you told me to do. You told me never to let you see my face."

The President said, "Anansi, I've had enough of your foolishness. I don't ever want to see you again, clothed or naked."

So Anansi went away. But the next day when he saw the President coming down the street he took his clothes off and put a fishnet over his head. When the President saw him he shouted, "Anansi, didn't I tell you I never wanted to see you again clothed or naked?" And Anansi said, "My President, I respect what you tell me. I'm not clothed and I'm not naked."

This time the President told him, "Anansi, if I ever catch you again on Haitian soil I'll have you shot."

So Anansi boarded a boat and sailed to Jamaica. He bought a pair of heavy shoes and put sand in them. Then he put the shoes on his feet and took another boat back to Haiti. When he arrived at Port-au-Prince⁰ he found the President standing on the pier.

"Anansi," the President said sternly, "Didn't I tell you that if I ever caught you on Haitian soil again I'd have you shot?"

"You told me that, Papa, and I respected what you said. I went to Jamaica and filled my shoes with sand. So I didn't disobey you because I'm now walking on English soil."⁰

–Reprinted from: Harold Courlander, *The Drum and the Hoe: Life and Lore of the Haitian People* (University of California Press, 1960).

Vocabulary

limekiln: furnace for making lime by burning limestone or shells

Port-au-Prince: capital of Haiti

English soil: Jamaica was still a colony of England when the story was told

READING

Anansi and the Magic Calabash

A FOLK TALE FROM ANTIGUA

One day Anansi was walking in the "bush"⁰ when he saw a calabash⁰ lying on the ground. He picked it up and admired it. The calabash suddenly spoke to Anansi, saying, "I am a magic calabash and I can make you any food you want." Anansi nearly dropped the calabash in fright, for whoever heard of a calabash that could speak? He spoke to the calabash, saying, "Was that you who just spoke?" "Yes," said the calabash. "What can you make?" asked Anansi. The calabash told him that it could make anything under the sun, so long as Anansi sang it a special song. Anansi then asked it to make him some fungi⁰ and saltfish⁰ after he had sung the special song.

Lo and behold, the calabash filled up with the fungi and saltfish, and even added some choba⁰ to go with it. Anansi was pleased as punch and filled his belly with the food. Then he washed the calabash and went home. When he got home, he put the calabash in his bedroom under his bed and told his wife and children not to go under the bed or he would beat them. The next day, Anansi went out all day and when he came home, he went into the bedroom, locked the door and sang the special song to the calabash. The calabash immediately filled up with fungi, saltfish, choba and this time, it added a few okras to

go with the meal. Anansi, greedy as he was, ate it all up and offered none to his family, who, meantime, were out in the other room eating their simple meal and wondering what was going on behind the closed door. Then Anansi cleaned the calabash and put it back under the bed.

Anansi's wife had heard the song quite clearly, and when Anansi left the next day, she went into the room, determined to find out what was under the bed. She picked up the calabash from under the bed and figured that if she sang the song she had heard she would soon know what had taken place in the room. She sang the song and to her shock and surprise the calabash filled up with food! She and the children ate their bellyfull, washed the calabash and put it back under the bed.

Anansi came home, went as usual to the calabash and sang the song, asking the calabash for his meal for the day; but nothing happened. He sang the song again, this time louder than before; but nothing happened. Finally, he asked the calabash, "What happened today, why you nar mek no food?" The calabash told him that it had already prepared the meal for the day, and couldn't make any more. Anansi got angry and smashed the calabash to bits.

The next day, he went out as usual and while walking through the bush he saw a whip. He took up the whip and was admiring it when the whip said, "I am a magic whip and I can perform for you." Without delay, Anansi said, "Perform for me then, whip!" The whip slipped out of his hands and began to beat poor Anansi. It followed him all the way home, beating him without mercy, for the whip could only perform in the custom it was used to. It beat Anansi until he said he was sorry for not sharing the food from the calabash with his wife and children. From that day, Anansi learned that he couldn't leave his family without food while he filled his own belly.

–Reprinted from: Althea V. Prince, "Anansi Folk Culture: An Expression of Caribbean Life," *Caribbean Review*, Vol. XIII, No.1, Winter 1984.

Vocabulary

bush: wild, wooded area

calabash: bowl made from a large gourd which is dried and hollowed out

fungi: cornmeal boiled to a thick paste

saltfish: fish (usually cod) preserved by drying and salting

choba: eggplant

READING

The Magic Hoe

A FOLK TALE FROM GHANA

In the beginning there was only one hoe in the world, and men worked their fields with a bush knife.[0] For the coming of the hoe to the Ashanti, Kotoko, the porcupine, is responsible, and Anansi, the spider, also played his part.

It is said that Kotoko and Anansi joined together to begin a new farm. When it was Anansi's turn to work, he took his family and went into the field and dug the earth with his bush knife. And when it was Kotoko's turn, he came to the field with a hoe. He raised his hoe and struck it on the earth, singing:

"Give me a hand, hoe of Kotoko, give me a hand! It is hot in the sun!"

The hoe leapt from Kotoko's hands and began to work in the field by itself. It cut up the earth over a great distance, and when night came, the porcupine said other words, and the hoe came to rest. When he went home, Kotoko took the hoe and hid it in his house.

But Kwaku Anansi, when he saw how the hoe labored, said: "Why do I break my back? I shall get this hoe and let it work for me." So early in the day, before the light came, Anansi went to Kotoko's house and stole the hoe from where it was hidden. He took it out to the field. He struck it on the earth and sang:

"Give me a hand, hoe of Kotoko, give me a hand! It is hot in the sun!"

The hoe began to work. It turned and cultivated the earth while Anansi sat in the shade and rested. Anansi said: "Whoever had a thing like this before?"

The hoe moved across the field. All the earth was newly turned. Anansi was satisfied. He said to the hoe: "Stop now; the field is done." But the hoe didn't stop, because Anansi didn't know the right word. It went right on hoeing. It hoed itself into the dense brush, and still Anansi couldn't stop it. It hoed itself to the edge of the sea, and still it would not stop. It went across the sea and came to the Country of the White People.

And there the people liked it and fashioned other hoes after it. And when they had made many, they brought some of them across the sea to the Ashanti people. Thus today among the Ashanti there are numerous hoes, and men use them instead of the bush knife when they have to till the earth.

–Reprinted from: Harold Courlander, *The Hat-Shaking Dance and Other Ashanti Tales from Ghana* (Harcourt Brace Jovanovich, 1957. Copyright 1957, 1985 by Harold Courlander.)

Vocabulary

bush knife: large knife used for agricultural work

READING
The Magic Hoe

A FOLK TALE FROM GEORGIA, USA

Bruh Rabbit and Bruh Wolf was always tryin' to git the best o' one another. Now Bruh Wolf he own a hoe and it work for crop all by itself.Bruh Wolf just say, "Swish," to it. Then he sit down in the field and the hoe do all the work.

Bruh Rabbit he want that hoe. He hide behind bush and watch how the wolf make it work. One day when the wolf away, Bruh Rabbit he steal the hoe. He go to he own field and he stand the hoe up and he say, "Swish." The hoe start to work. It work and work. 'Fore long the crop is done finish. Then rabbit want hoe to stop, and he call out and he call out but hoe keep right on workin'. Bruh Rabbit don't know what word to say to stop it. Pretty soon the hoe cut down all Bruh Rabbit's winter crop and still it keep on workin' and workin'. Bruh Rabbit wring he hands. Everything he has is gone.

Just then Bruh Wolf come along and he laugh and laugh out loud when he see how Bruh Rabbit steal he hoe and how it done ruin all the crop. Bruh Rabbit he keep callin' out, "Swish, swish," and the hoe go faster and faster. When he see Bruh Wolf, he ax 'im to make the hoe stop. Bruh Wolf won't say nothin' at all 'cause he mad that Bruh Rabbit steal he hoe. Then after a time he say, "Slow boy," and the hoe stop workin'. Then Bruh Wolf he pick up he hoe and carry him home.

–Reprinted from: *Drums and Shadows: Survival Studies Among the Georgia Coastal Negroes*, edited by the Georgia Writers' Project (University of Georgia Press, 1940).

When I was little, my life was full of people anxious to tell me Anancy stories, to help me clap to short rhymes and to recite long story poems for my entertainment. For I grew up in the country, where the pace of life was slow and where night came as soon as lamps were lit. Even when there was radio, the station was in operation for only a short time in the evening. Stories and poems are therefore some of the best parts of my earliest memories and I have this terrible fear that there are children listening to radio and looking at TV who will never know half the stories and poems I knew when I was their age.

–Velma Pollard, Jamaican educator
From *Anansesem: A Collection of Caribbean Folk Tales, Legends and Poems for Juniors*

UNIT TWO: Our Jamaican Heritage
TEACHER GUIDE

▶ **OBJECTIVES**

Students will:

1. Describe six customs associated with Jamaican rural life

2. Identify examples of African and European traditions which have influenced Jamaican culture

▶ **QUESTIONS FOR DISCUSSION**

1. What percentage of Jamaicans are either completely or partly of African descent? Why is this so? What other ethnic and national "roots" do some Jamaicans have? (Refer to "A Brief History of Jamaica").

2. Why didn't Claude McKay and his schoolmates have an accurate idea of snow? How do the Jamaican seasons differ from the ones you are familiar with? What is a "rainy season?"

3. How did the people in McKay's village make their living? Why were the hurricanes a disaster for them?

4. What aspects of Jamaican life was Claude McKay proud of?

5. In what ways is Leonard Barrett the product of two traditions? Why is his African heritage important to him?

6. Why was there such excitement in the Ghanaian market place when Barrett said "dokono?"

7. In what ways has African culture affected Jamaican life? Give examples.

8. Think about your own family's background and cultural traditions. Which customs have continued over generations in your family? What do you know about their origins?

▶ **SUGGESTED ACTIVITIES**

1. [Middle school students] Students illustrate any portion of the Claude McKay reading.

2. Students locate Ghana and Jamaica on a map. Select some students to report on various aspects of Ashanti culture as it exists today in Ghana.

3. Divide the class into three groups. Each group will take one of the following topics: 1) agriculture and food 2) language 3) proverbs. Each group creates a bulletin board display about Jamaican culture, focusing on its topic.

4. Discuss the meaning of one of the proverbs with the class. Then divide the students into groups. Each group will explain in their own words the meaning of the rest of the sayings. They may also suggest American proverbs or proverbs from another culture that express similar ideas.

▶ **RESOURCES**

1. Olive Senior, A-Z *of Jamaican Heritage* (Heinemann, 1983). An illustrated guide to Jamaican people, places, customs, foods, etc., arranged encyclope-dia-style. Available from Heinemann.

2. Two anthologies suitable for senior high students and undergraduates:

• Margaret E. Crahan and Franklin W. Knight, eds., *Africa and the Caribbean: The Legacies of a Link* (Johns Hopkins University Press, 1980).

• Sidney W. Mintz and Sally Price, eds., *Caribbean Contours* (Johns Hopkins University Press, 1985).

INTRODUCTION
Our Jamaican Heritage

The cultural heritage of Jamaicans draws on many influences, but the most important are Africa and Europe. Ninety percent of Jamaicans are of African or African/European descent. The blending of these two traditions is fundamental to Jamaican life.

The Africans who came to Jamaica brought their languages, customs and religious beliefs with them. Many of these survived the slavery experience to become part of Jamaican culture. African influences are evident today in Jamaican speech, foods, folk beliefs and religion; in music and dance; and in family and community life.

At the same time, the British imposed their own language and culture on the island during 300 years of colonial rule. The main vehicles for this influence were the Protestant and Catholic churches and the educational system. Many clergy, school principals and teachers, at least initially, were non-Jamaicans. They encouraged Afro-Jamaicans to adopt European values and ways.

Jamaicans did embrace many aspects of British culture. But they also struggled to hold on to and defend those parts of their culture which were African. This dual influence is evident in the readings by Claude McKay and Leonard Barrett.

Claude McKay is Jamaica's best-known novelist and poet. Born in 1890, he migrated to New York in 1912 and became a leading figure in the Black literary movement known as the Harlem Renaissance. In *My Green Hills of Jamaica*, McKay describes his childhood village in Jamaica as he remembers it from around 1900. It is a sentimental look backward, describing a harmonious and peaceful world.

McKay's later writing expresses his pride in blackness and critiques racism. But at the time *My Green Hills* was written, there was as yet no broad-based movement in Jamaica to recognize the country's African heritage. Accordingly, McKay's account reflects more strongly the European influences on Jamaican life.

In the 1960s, after Jamaica became independent, increasing numbers of Jamaicans became interested in their African roots. The African-Caribbean Institute, part of the Institute of Jamaica, was created to disseminate information about the African cultural heritage in Jamaica and the Caribbean.

Leonard Barrett, a professor at Temple University in Philadelphia, grew up in rural Jamaica. To gain insight into his heritage, he traveled to Ghana, West Africa. In *The Sun and the Drum*, Barrett describes how his family's and community's traditions reflected their African past.

READING
My Green Hills of Jamaica

BY CLAUDE MCKAY

My Village

My village was beautiful, sunshiny, sparsely populated. It was set upon a hill. Except when it rained or was foggy, it was always bathed by the sun. The hills came like chains from the other villages—James Hill, Taremont, Croft's Hill, Frankfield, and Ballad's River. They came to form a center in Sunny Ville.⁰

The village was set, something like a triangle, between two streams. The parochial or dirt road along which it grew on both sides jutted off abruptly from the main macadamised⁰ road. We were about twenty-one families living between those two streams—one so large we called it a river and the other just a tributary which further down emptied itself into a large river.

The road was red, very red. I remember during the rainy season how that red clay would cake up on the legs and feet of the old folks going to work their patches of land, and kids going to school.

On Sunday during that kind of weather, the peasant men went to church with their shoes slung over their shoulders, and the peasant women carrying theirs either on their arms or on their heads. When they got to the brook near the church, they would wash their feet, put on their shoes, and step gingerly on the grass leading to the church doors.

What used to tickle us chil-

Artist: *Albert Huie*

dren was the quietness of the church and the squeaking of the shoes of our elders as they walked down the aisle to the front benches.

Nearly all the women wore brightly colored Madras hand-kerchiefs which were always stiffly starched. Some of them were knotted upon their heads in the kind of turban that is so fashionable in America today, and others were tied under the neck like American school girls wear them.

One of the things that delighted me most as a child was the way their frocks⁰ rustled as the women walked down the aisle of the church. I am not sure of just what material they were made, but it must have been what Americans call taffeta. Nearly every well-fixed peasant woman had a silk frock.

The women were vain because when they were stepping over the stones which had been placed in the stream for the people to cross, they would lift their silk frocks almost waist high, displaying their beautiful white petticoats. Some of these petticoats were filled with beautiful lace, much of it hand-crocheted and beautiful hand-embroidering—skills at which the peasant women were very proficient. They always kept these white petticoats stiffly starched.

The rainy season in Jamaica started either in September or October. It lasted about six weeks. This was our coldest season ... sometimes we had to burn wood and bring coal into the house. Some of the peasants used charcoal. We would put the coals in kerosene tins, which were cut down by half and that would generate a fine heat.

In our elementary school books we read stories of English, German and Dutch children playing in the snow. I especially remember the pic-

tures of the Dutch children in their colored scarves and wooden shoes; but we never really had a correct idea of what snow was. The nearest thing we had to snow was the hail that fell with the rains in the rainy season. They were large pieces of hail, sometimes as long as four inches and about an inch wide. The nearest thing to describe the large hailstones of Jamaica would be the small icicles in America.

We children were quite oblivious of the damage that the hail did to the crops. When it came we youngsters would strip naked and dart out in to the rain to pick up hailstones. We used to make a special drink with them—a cold drink with sugar and lemon and sometimes syrup.

Sometimes the rainy season came in with a fierce hurricane which would sweep everything before it, uprooting the strongest trees and destroying the best crops of bananas, sugar cane, corn and yams.⁰ Sometimes it knocked down the peasants' huts. Everything was flattened down like reeds by a wind.

We kids just loved the hurricane yet the aftermath was sheer misery. With all the best crops destroyed and the fruit trees uprooted, the villages were faced with starvation. Somehow I recall that we always used to pull through. Those peasants who had money saved up (and most of them did) used to buy barrels and bags of flour from the town. We would mix it with corn meal and make all kinds of

food—johnny cakes, dumplings and mush.

The hurricanes did not come regularly—sometimes for five or six years we did not have one and again suddenly we might have two within a period of two years.

Most of the time there was hardly any way of telling the seasons. To us in Jamaica there were only two seasons—the rainy season and the dry season. We had no idea of Spring, Summer, Autumn and Winter like the peoples of northern lands. Springtime however we did know by the new and lush burgeoning of grasses and the blossoming of trees although we had blooms all the year round. The mango tree was especially significant of Spring because it was one of the few trees that used to shed its leaves. Then in Springtime the new leaves sprouted—very tender, a kind of sulphur brown as if they had been singed by fire. Soon afterwards the white blossoms came out and we knew that we would be eating juicy mangoes by August.

My youth in Jamaica was not unhappy. In our village we were poor enough but very proud peasants. We had plenty to eat. We had enough to wear, a roof against the rain, and beautiful spreading trees to shade us from the sun ...

Time of Planting

Up there in the hills the peasants had a very primitive way of cultivating the soil; but it sufficed all the same for their needs. Their main implements were the machete, the hoe, the fork and the pick-axe—but the machete was the most indispensable of all.

Machete is a Spanish word. It resembles a very large and broad knife. The natives use it for cutting down trees, except very large trees where the axe is used. They use it for clearing the soil and for every conceivable thing in the way of cutting. In the far regions they even use it for a kitchen tool—for cutting yams and potatoes and peeling them to cook.

When planting time comes around, a peasant who has a large lot of land will be helped by other peasants especially in clearing the soil. The land is first cleared by the machetes and then two or three days later the shrubs and grass which were cleared are burned. It is a very light burning and we children used to revel in the blue smoke curling up to the skies.

When the British started to send us agricultural instructors to show the peasants how to till the soil, these men protested against the burning of the debris. They said that the debris would enrich the soil and should be plowed under. Well, some of the peasants followed their advice and when they did their planting, the leaves of what they had planted were consumed by worms as soon as they had grown a few inches. Those who insisted on burning this debris found that their planting had developed very healthily. The agricultural instructors made their mistakes.

I remember one of them telling a peasant that the young cocoa plant that he had uprooted would not grow. The peasant insisted that it would and planted it. The next year when the instructor returned, he found a flourishing cocoa tree.

Our peasants did their clearing of the land and planting accompanied by much singing. These songs were very different and were known to us as "Jamma Songs," or "Field Songs." They were led off by a leader and the rest of the men joined in the chorus. They were very much like the "Calypso" songs of today, and some of them faintly resembled the popular flamenco songs of Morocco and Spain.

At noontime, when the men were tired and hungry the women had plenty of food ready for them—yams, boiled plantains[0], cocos[0], plenty of fish, chunks of meat which they ate and washed down with a beverage made from bitter oranges and home-made brown sugar. Such was the way of clearing the land and planting it. Today one peasant was helped by the other peasants and the next day it was another peasant. So it went round and round until every peasant had had his land cleared and planted ...

Artist: Michelle Gibbs

Country People

People who are born and grow up in large cities have a tendency to imagine that people from small towns and villages are naturally stupid and unintelligent. There is no greater fallacy. Personally I believe that the masses of the cities are woefully less intelligent than people who make up the population of a country town or village. The country and small town man may not be as slickly dressed but somehow he does use his brains to think. I have known so many city people from truck driver to professor who just cannot think at all.

If there was ever anything that could be called a backward place it was my home up there in the Clarendon hills. We were twenty-two miles away from the nearest railroad station. A few neighbors subscribed for the weekly *Jamaica Times* which everybody read. There was also the mission library to which every intelligent barefooted boy had access, and there were many of us. We read such magazines as *The Spectator*, *The Nineteenth Century*, *Answers*, *The Windsor*, and the weekly edition of *The Times*, many English provincial papers as well as *The Outlook*, *The Argosy*, the famous *New York Herald*, the Deadwood Dick detective stories and other magazines and newspapers which I don't remember from America.

They were all good and bad thrown together and we young people read indiscriminately. We had Marie Corelli, Mrs. Humphrey Ward, Miss Braddon, Mrs. Gaskell, Sheldon's *In His Steps*, which was a very wonderful book for us kids who were being trained to be model colonial Christians. Most famous of all the books was Mrs. Henry Wood's *East Lynne*. I remember that I read passages from it to my mother and cried in her lap and she cried too.

Then we had a literary debating society where we discussed such things as Chinese and East Indian immigration into Jamaica and why these people were forced to leave their homes to work for so much less than the Jamaica native whose wages were just a pittance anyhow. We debated also about the British empire and its role in the world comparing it to the Spanish empire. Every school kid has some knowledge of the Spanish Armada. We also knew that Jamaica was Spanish before it was taken by the English.

We still have many of the Spanish names which were to us so romantic, like St. Jago de la Vega, Río Cobre, Río Minho, Montego Bay, Santa Cruz and Savanna la Mar. We had also the titillating names of our well integrated Jewish population who had come to us from Spain and Portugal at the beginning of the sixteenth century. Such names as de Cordova, de Lindo, Delgado, Delevante, Del Ano, De Paseo, Demendez, D'Aguilar, Enriquez, Morales and Andrade. Just like the English and Scotch and some of our Negroes they had shops in the city and towns, and they were also landed proprietors and good politicians. In everything that was done in the island they took a part, and there was no thought of discriminating against them or against other white people; or Chinese, or East Indians[0], mulattoes[0] and Negroes who had arisen to the position where they could take part in the management of the island's affairs. In spite of its poverty, my island of Jamaica was like a beautiful garden in human relationships ...

–Abridged from: Claude McKay, *My Green Hills of Jamaica* (Heinemann, 1979).

Vocabulary

Sunny Ville: McKay has given a fictional name to his village

macadamized: paved

frocks: dresses

yam: starchy root vegetable

plantain: vegetable resembling a large banana, which is cooked before eating

coco: starchy root vegetable

East Indians: people from India and their descendents

mulatto: of mixed African/European descent

READING
African Roots of My Jamaican Heritage

BY LEONARD BARRETT

My interest in African traditions goes back deep into the bushes of my Jamaica homeland. It was there that, in my youth, I detected two distinct streams of culture intermingling. My father was of pure African stock and my mother was mixed; in Jamaican "talk" she was a high mulatto[0].

Little was known of my father's father, although there is no doubt about his African origin. Much, however, was known of his mother, Sarbah, and she was frequently referred to during my childhood. Apparently she wore an African tribal mark on her cheek, and she was probably a late arrival from the Gold Coast[0] to Jamaica.

On my mother's side, little was ever said of her father. He was an Englishman, married to a light brown Jamaican. The relationship seems to have been a strange one. He died before I was born, and all I can remember is that almost the entire village was once his property, but he lost it because of his love for Jamaican rum ...

Even as a child I could feel a slight social and cultural conflict between my mother's relatives and my father's. All the members of the family on my mother's side were practicing Christians, whereas those on my father's side shunned Christianity. My father's relatives were all

followers of the native Pukumina[0] religion, which was a modified version of the African Kumina[0] cult.

Although my mother was a mulatto, she was in no way influenced by her father. Like many mulattos, she was Caucasian[0] in her features but African in culture. She was a member of the Christian church with a fair knowledge of the Bible and the do's and don'ts of her church, but her daily life was lived in the folk atmosphere of Jamaican "bush[0]." Sunday morning meant going to church to sing English hymns, but Monday through Saturday meant living in the tightly-knit Jamaican community with its African lore, beliefs, and practices. To her, there was no contradiction in this way of life, so it was from my mother's behavior that I became aware quite early that two cultural traditions were operating in our lives.

I used to observe this especially at Christmas time. On Christmas Eve nights, special drinks were bought and prepared for the Christmas festivities. At twelve o'clock, which was indicated by the crowing of the roosters in the neighborhood (in those days we had no clocks), my mother would go to the east window of the house, pour a cup of the drink outside and say, "Happy Christmas, my

Ashanti carved wooden door panel from Ghana.

relatives and loved ones." That little ceremony completed, we all eagerly shared in the festivities. Few homes in the neighborhood would celebrate the season without this ritual. It was not until years later when I left Jamaica and began to study African history and culture that I found out that my mother's ritual was the pouring of an African libation to the departed dead.

In addition, there were many other customs which it seemed

to me were neither Western nor Christian, but an indispensable part of our culture. I later understood these customs to be a part of our African heritage which served to identify us as a people of two cultures: the first, African and a part of our identity; the second, a thin layer of the European slavemaster's culture that filtered down to us through the churches and the mission schools[0].

My Heritage

I was born in the village of Shrewsbury in the Parish of Saint Elizabeth, in the foothills just above the coastal town of Black River, the capital of the parish. Saint Elizabeth has a rich history of slave rebellion. It was in this parish that the famous Acheampong resided with his roving bands of Maroons[0]. His name is still preserved in the present Maroon community known as "Accompong Town."

Although various African peoples entered Jamaica, the most dominant were the Ashanti-Fanti[0], who were closely related in origin and language. They were followed by the Yoruba-Ibo[0] peoples whose influences can still be found in the islands. All others seemed to have merged their identity, language, and religious customs with these two.

Despite the strong Yoruba-Ibo complex in some places, the Ashanti-Fanti culture-complex dominated Jamaica as a whole. Almost all the names of Maroon chiefs and generals that have

come down to us were either Ashanti or Fanti in origin. Thus we have names like Cudjoe, Quao, Nana Acheampong, Kwaku, and Takyi—all Akan[0] names, the day-names of the Akan peoples of Ghana, formerly the Gold Coast.

In my community there seems to have been a mixture of Yorubas whose names can still be found among the older generation. Names like Oni, Obi, Yubi, and Boki are still common but are now dying out.

Language

The official language of Jamaica is English, and Jamaican intellectuals take pride in speaking the Queen's English[0] faultlessly. It is the language of the schools, the mass media, commerce, and technology. But in Jamaica, English is a second language, a foreign language that must be learned. The lingua franca of the Jamaican people is referred to as " Jamaican dialect" or "patois," which is a mixture of English, Spanish, and various African languages. The dominant African language in the dialect is Twi—the language of the Akan peoples of Ghana, formerly the Gold Coast.

This mixture remains the standard means of communication to the present day. In my case, I knew no standard English until I entered elementary school at the age of 8. I can still recall how often we were flogged by the teachers for speaking non-standard English (patois) ...

I have already referred to names of people which in my

youth were unmistakably African, both Akan and Yoruba, in sound and meaning. Although this custom is now dying out, there are many people still alive with these names, and they are still assigning names of African origin to their children. For example, my first name was Cudjoe, for those persons born on Monday. There were many Cudjoes in my neighborhood; in particular there was Cudjoe Porter, an old man who spent much time instructing me and recalling many stories and folk tales. Other names included Cubennah, for a man born on Tuesday; Juba for a Monday-born woman; Abba for a Thursday-born woman; Bakkar for a first-born; Pheba and Efi for a Friday-born woman; Quasheba for a Sunday-born woman.

The language of my community is also rich in descriptive terms which have no other origin but African. A child who is slow to walk as a result of the nutritional deficiency which

Engraved calabash design from Benin

results in rickets is known as a *bafan*. In Twi it is the name of a child who fails to walk between the ages of 2 and 7. The name is used for all young people with a leg defect and, in my community, to be called a *bafan* is a serious embarrassment.

A person who is mentally dull is called *bobo* from the Twi word *booboo*, meaning a foolish person—one who is phlegmatic and dull. Some persons in my community bear that name permanently. A very obese person is amusingly referred to as *buffu-buffu*, which is a corruption of the Twi word *bofoo*, meaning clumsy, swollen, fat and fleshy.

A contentious person is known as a *kaskas*, from the Twi word *kasakasa*. A person who is disorderly in appearance and living conditions is referred to as *chaka-chaka*. The same characteristic is known in Ghana as *takataka*. A person who performs a piece-of-a-job (involving the use of implements) or does his work badly or half-heartedly is said to *nyaka-nyaka* his work. This is the perfect Twi translation and is used in present-day Ghana. On the contrary, a person who is meticulous or fastidious in appearance and habits is *fenky-fenky*. The word has the same meaning in Accra, the capital of Ghana.

Food

Let us turn to the subject of food and the names of the things eaten in my community. First I will give a personal experience to illustrate the close connection between my village and West Africa. As a boy, my mother often cooked a specialty for us which was always a welcome change in the village menu. She would soak or boil dried corn-on-the-cob, then grate or pound it into flour in a mortar.[0] She would mix the flour with sugar, nutmeg, and salt, adding a little wheat flour to thicken it. She then cut the batter into one-pound pieces, wrapped each piece in banana

Proverbs

Of the many thousands of proverbs gathered among the Ashanti, there are hundreds that have turned up in Jamaica in their original forms and many more that have been modified to fit New World conditions. The following are only a few examples which may be heard in my community and which were quoted to me by my kinsfolk.

Ashanti (in English translation)

- It is the Supreme Being who brushes the flies off the tailless animal.
- The white-tailed one (the black Columbus monkey) says: What is in my cheek is not mine, but what has gone into my belly that is my very own.
- When you have quite crossed the river, you say that the crocodile has a lump on its snout.
- When a number of mice dig a hole it does not get deep.
- It is the water which stands calm and silent that drowns.
- It is the fool's sheep that breaks loose twice.
- When one does not know how to dance he says, "The drum is not sounding sweetly."

Jamaican

- When cow tail cut off God-a-mighty brush fly.
- Monkey say wha' in him mout, no-fe him, but wha' in him belly a fe-him.

- No cuss alligator long mouth till you cross ribber.
- Too much rat nebber dig good hole.

- Noisy ribber no drown nobody.

- One time no fool, but two time fool him a dam fool.
- When man can't dance him say music no good.

Catfish design in carved ivory from Nigeria

leaves, and put them in boiling water for an hour, after which she cooled and served one to each of us. The name of this morsel is *dokono*.

In 1969, on my first trip to Africa, our party stopped at the Koromantyn Market at the foot of the famous Koromantyn Castle from which most Jamaican slaves embarked on their Atlantic journey to Jamaica. Walking in the market, I came upon a woman with a stall of the same banana leaf preparation. I pointed to it and said "dokono!" The woman, who spoke no English, was startled. She ran and called a man who spoke English and Twi. On their way back to me, the woman was frantically explaining something to him. He finally caught up with me and asked how I knew that the items were dokono. I told him that my mother used to make them and referred to them by that name in Jamaica. In a few minutes I was in the midst of a noisy admiring crowd of old men and women all talking to one another. Some came close, hugging my hands in a most caressing manner. The gentlemen explained to me that the elders were giving me an African

welcome because I was the son of an ancestor who was sold in slavery. He further explained that the name "dokono" was a Fanti word which was used only among the people of the Cape Coast, and that the knowledge of the name among my family was sufficient evidence that my grandparents came from the region.

Along with dokono, there are many other names traceable to the Gold Coast, such as the word *fufu*. In Africa, and particularly Ghana, the word is used for the combination of yam[o], plantain[o], and cassava[o] which is boiled and pounded into a tough dough and used in soup. Using the fingers, one works the dough into small pieces, dipping it into either soup or a sauce and then eating it. One finds the same name, method of preparation, and manner of consumption in many parts of Saint Elizabeth.

–Abridged from: Leonard Barrett, *The Sun and the Drum: African Roots in Jamaican Folk Tradition* (Sangster's Book Stores and Heinemann Educational Books Ltd., 1976)

Vocabulary

mulatto: brown-skinned person of mixed African/European descent

high mulatto: person with very light brown skin

Gold Coast: former name of Ghana

Pukumina (or Pocomania): Jamaican cult mixing Christian fundamentalism with

African religious customs. Worship combines Bible reading and prayer with singing, dancing, drumming and spirit possession.

Kumina: religious cult of African origins, involving possession by the spirits of ancestors

Caucasian: white

bush: rural areas

mission schools: schools run by missionaries sent by churches based outside Jamaica

maroons: escaped slaves who set up independent communities and fought guerrilla wars against the slaveowners

Ashanti: a West African people living in modern Ghana

Fanti: a West African people living in modern Ghana

Yoruba: a West African people living in modern Nigeria

Ibo: a West African people living in modern Nigeria

Akan: group of related West African peoples, including the Ashanti and Fanti

Queen's English: English spoken by educated people

mortar: container to hold food while it is pounded by hand

yam: starchy root vegetable

plantain: vegetable resembling a large banana, which is cooked before eating

cassava: starchy root vegetable, also called manioc or yuca

UNIT THREE: The Marcus Garvey Movement
TEACHER GUIDE

▶ **OBJECTIVES**

Students will:

1. Define the concept of Pan-Africanism

2. Evaluate the ideas and achievements of Marcus Garvey

3. Analyze how Garvey created links between people of African descent in the United States and the Caribbean

▶ **QUESTIONS FOR DISCUSSION**

1. What was the situation in Africa in the early twentieth century? What was the status of Black people in the Caribbean? In North America? How did this affect Garvey?

2. What is Pan-Africanism? Is there a relationship between African independence and the rights of people of African descent
in the Caribbean and the United States? Describe that relationship.

3. What was the Universal Negro Improvement Association? What did it do? What were the major points of Garvey's message? Why did many people respond positively to this message?

5. In what ways were Garvey's ideas controversial? Why did some people reject his views?

6. What do you think was Garvey's most important achievement?

7. How did the British colonial authorities and the U.S. government try to hinder Garvey's movement? Why do you think they did this?

8. What might Garvey say about the status of African-Americans if he were alive today?

9. Have you ever been to a wake or funeral? How did it compare to the rituals described in "Burying Miss 'Mando"?

10. Why do you think Miss 'Mando was a loyal follower of Garvey?

11. What is the meaning of the phrase "a dream deferred but not forgotten" in the context of this story?

▶ **SUGGESTED ACTIVITIES**

1. Divide the class into two parts. One group will research and report on the status of Black people in the United States and the Caribbean after abolition. Consider: voting and other civil rights; segregation; economic conditions; racist attitudes and violence against Blacks.

The other group will report on the colonial division of Africa. Which European countries took control of which parts of Africa? What were their motives?

What were some of the consequences?

After the reports have been prepared, each group will share its findings with the class. Conclude with a discussion of how these conditions inspired the rise of the Pan-African movement and Garvey.

2. Garvey's UNIA had many members in the United States. You may be lucky enough to find a former member—probably in his or her eighties or older—who lives in your community and has memories to share. Students can record an interview and edit it into a form to be shared with others. Possibilities include a bulletin board display at school or in a community center, an article in a local newspaper, or a radio interview. Be creative!

3. The class finds out about other Pan-Africanists who came before Garvey and created a foundation for his work, e.g. Dr. Robert Love, W.E.B. Du Bois, Edward Blyden, J.J. Thomas, Henry Sylvester Williams, George Padmore, Henry McNeil Turner. Each student should prepare a one-page report on one of these men.

4. The class researches the role of women in the Garvey movement, including the contributions of Garvey's wives, Amy Ashwood Garvey and Amy Jacques Garvey. Be sure to consult Amy Jacques Garvey's book *Garvey and Garveyism* (see Resources).

5. [Middle school students] Students make a poster or write a song, poem or story expressing some aspect of Garvey's ideas. They may support or reject these ideas, as long as they show that they understand them. An alternative is to draw a picture illustrating a scene from the story "Burying Miss 'Mando."

▶ **RESOURCES**

1. There is a large literature on Pan-Africanism and Marcus Garvey. Some sources include:

• John Henrik Clarke, ed., *Marcus Garvey and the Vision of Africa* (Vintage Books, 1974).

• Robert Hill, *The Marcus Garvey and Universal Negro Improvement Association Papers* (University of California Press, Los Angeles, 1983). Two volumes of primary documents.

• Amy Jacques-Garvey, *Garvey and Garveyism* (Collier Books, 1970). Account of Garvey's life and political movement by his widow.

• Amy Jacques-Garvey, ed., *Philosophy and Opinions of Marcus Garvey* (Atheneum, 1982). Garvey's writings and speeches.

• Nathan Irvin Huggins, *Harlem Renaissance* (Oxford University Press, 1971). Garvey in the context of Black intellectual and political life of the early 20th century.

• Mary Lawler, *Marcus Garvey: Black Nationalist Leader* (Chelsea House Pub., 1988). Text suitable for middle school students. Illustrated with historical photographs.

• Rupert Lewis, *Marcus Garvey: Anti-Colonial Champion* (Africa World Press, 1988). Detailed historical account, focusing on Garvey's work in Jamaica.

• Rupert Lewis and Patrick Bryan, eds., *Garvey: His Work and Impact* (University of the West Indies, 1989). Examines issues of race, Garveyism and Pan-Africanism in light of contemporary realities. Available from UWI Publishers Association, P.O. Box 42, Mona, Kingston 7, Jamaica.

• Tony Martin, *Marcus Garvey, Hero. A First Biography.* (Majority Press, 1983).

• Tony Sewell, *Garvey's Children: The Legacy of Marcus Garvey* (Africa World Press, 1990). Explores Garvey's influence on political and cultural figures such as Malcolm X, Kwame Nkrumah, and Bob Marley.

• Jeannette Smith-Irvin, *Marcus Garvey's Footsoldiers of the Universal Negro Improvement Association* (Africa World Press, 1989). Interviews with seven men and women who were active in the UNIA.

Garvey supporters line Harlem streets for the parade preceding the UNIA's convention in 1924.

INTRODUCTION
The Marcus Garvey Movement

During the 1800s, the harsh experience of Blacks in the United States fueled dreams of an independent, Black-ruled nation in Africa. Some religious and community leaders, notably Bishop Henry McNeil Turner of the African Methodist Episcopal (AME) Church, called for American Blacks to return to Africa to found such a nation. Various repatriation schemes resulted in the settlement of some Black emigrants in Liberia.

This vision of a free, independent Africa stood in stark contrast to the reality of colonial conquest. By 1912 the European powers had completed their division of the continent. Only two African countries, Liberia and Ethiopia, were still independent of foreign control. They became symbols of freedom and dignity to many Black people in the West. A movement called Ethiopianism developed among Black churchgoers, holding Ethiopia up as a spiritual home. Missionaries of the AME Church from the United States helped spread Ethiopianist ideas in the Caribbean and South Africa.

Ethiopianism helped provide a basis for Pan-Africanism, a political movement which urged people of African descent to unite and work for common goals. Activists convened six Pan-African conferences between 1900 and 1945, calling for self-rule for Africa and full civil rights for Blacks in white-ruled societies.

Caribbean people played a major role in the movement. Edward Wilmot Blyden, who migrated from the Virgin Islands to become a government official in Liberia, urged Caribbean Blacks to settle in Africa. J.J. Thomas, a Trinidadian, wrote a book refuting the racist theories of the day. Henry Sylvester Williams, also born in Trinidad, helped convene the first Pan-African Conference in London. In Jamaica, Dr. Robert Love helped Williams set up branches of the Pan-African Association.

The Impact of Garvey

It was Marcus Garvey, however, who succeeded in building a mass organization based on Pan-African ideas. Garvey was born in Jamaica in 1887 of a humble peasant family. From 1910 to 1912 he traveled in Central and South America, where he saw Blacks, many of them Caribbean emigrants, laboring under harsh conditions.

From 1912 to 1914 he lived in

Marcus Garvey

London and worked on a Pan-African newspaper. Upon returning to Jamaica in 1916, Garvey formed the Universal Negro Improvement Association (UNIA). The UNIA's goal was to unite Blacks into a proud, strong nation. As part of this dream, it advocated the return of a vanguard to Africa to help free the continent from colonial rule. The UNIA anthem, "Ethiopia, Thou Land of Our Fathers," reflected the ideas of the Ethiopianist movement.

Garvey initially met with frustration in Jamaica. The

middle class, and even many workers, feared his strident emphasis on race. He moved to the United States, where his ideas caught fire among the thousands of southern Blacks who had moved north to industrial cities such as New York, Detroit and Philadelphia. The UNIA took root in New York City's Harlem section. It established branches in 40 countries, and claimed two million dues-paying members.

Women played a strong role in the UNIA. Amy Ashwood Garvey, Garvey's first wife, co-founded the organization and helped organize women within it. Inside the UNIA, a unit of "Black Cross Nurses" performed social and community work, and their activism provided a base for early Black feminists in both Jamaica and the United States. Garvey's second wife, Amy Jacques Garvey, documented his life's work in *The Philosophy and Opinions of Marcus Garvey.*

The UNIA ran a network of centers called Liberty Halls, which provided social services and credit to Black communities. To promote economic self-reliance, the organization launched a chain of Black-owned small businesses. The most ambitious project was a steamship venture, the Black Star Line, intended to link Black peoples around the world.

Although the Black Star Line was a financial failure, the UNIA was the most successful grassroots organization of Black people in history. In 1920, some 25,000 people crowded into New York's Madison Square Garden

Amy Jacques Garvey

for the UNIA's first international convention. The convention produced a "bill of rights," demanding that the world's governments recognize the UNIA as representative of all Black people. It called for Africa to be freed from colonial rule, and for full political rights for Blacks everywhere.

The UNIA's main strongholds were in the United States and the Caribbean, but branches existed in Europe, Canada, Australia, Latin America and South Africa. In the Caribbean, the movement cut across colonial lines. There were branches in Jamaica, Trinidad and the other English-speaking territories; in Spanish-speaking Cuba, Puerto Rico and the Dominican Republic; in French-speaking Haiti; and in Dutch-speaking Suriname. Caribbean emigrants in Panama, Costa Rica, Honduras, Columbia, Guatemala and Nicaragua also formed branches of the UNIA.

As the movement gained strength, the U.S. government and colonial authorities in the

Caribbean acted to suppress it. Garvey's newspaper, the *Negro World*, was banned in many places, and active followers of Garvey were denied entry to many Caribbean colonies. In 1925, U.S. federal authorities arrested Garvey on trumped-up mail fraud charges and imprisoned him for two years in Atlanta. He was deported to Jamaica in 1927.

Garvey returned to a triumphant hero's welcome from Jamaican workers. He spoke in Kingston to packed houses. He formed the People's Political Party, the first party in Jamaica's history to oppose colonial rule. The party demanded reforms to benefit the poor, such as a minimum wage, an 8-hour work day, and land reform. Garvey also formed Jamaica's first labor union, the Workingman and Labourers Association.

Garvey sought election to the Jamaican legislative council. But in the Jamaica of the 1930s, poor people did not have the right to vote. Many middle-class and upper-class Jamaicans still rejected Garvey's ideas, and he lost the election. His health declined, and the Depression eroded the financial base of the UNIA. In 1935 he left for England, where he spent the last years of his life.

The UNIA did not survive as a mass-based organization. But Garvey's success in moving millions of men and women to a common dream was an enduring achievement. His ideas laid the foundation upon which many other Black leaders built in the years to come.

READING
"A Great Nation of Black Men"

MARCUS GARVEY SPEAKS TO JAMAICANS AT THE WARD THEATER IN
KINGSTON, JAMAICA, DECEMBER 18, 1927

The Universal Negro Improvement Association was founded in 1914 after my experience of travel in South America, in Central America, in all the West Indian⁰ islands and in Europe, seeing well the need for greater unity amongst the Black people of the world ...

You all know how the different West Indians despise each other, how the Jamaican despises the Barbadian and the Barbadian despises the Jamaican and all the other islanders hate each other to the point where in America, they would not assimilate. They worked against each other and the American Negroes worked against them and they were all pulling against each other.

It was because of that urge to unity that I came back from England to Jamaica and founded here in 1914 the Universal Negro Improvement Association. So when I arrived in Harlem⁰ in New York the Jamaicans thought that I had come to speak to them especially. But I disappointed them and I spoke to the Negro people, and I told the Negro people of Harlem, including Americans, West Indians—Negroes all—the truth of their history. I told them that we were one, the same branch of one human family; that it was only a question of accident that made some of us American Negroes and others West Indian Negroes.

I told them that the slave trade as it was insti-tuted, brought from Africa Negroes, millions of them, against their wish and distributed them in the British colonies of the Western world without any regard for geographical boundaries, from whence they came or to the places to which they were taken. If it suited the whim and caprice of the slave master in Virginia, I told them, or in any part of America, the African husband would be sold in Virginia, and if it suited the whim and caprice of the slave master in Jamaica, the African wife would be sold in Jamaica and the two who were one would go away separated against their wish or will ...

Therefore the American Negroes and the West Indian Negroes are one, and they are relics of the great African race which was brought into the Western world and kept here for 300 years. I told them in Harlem that it was my duty to reunite the Negroes of the Western world with the Negroes of Africa, to make a great nation of Black men ...

Vocabulary

West Indian: Caribbean

Harlem: New York City neighborhood which was a center of African-American culture during the 1920s and 1930s. Emigrants from the Caribbean also settled there during that period.

READING
Remembering Marcus Garvey

ARNOLD L. CRAWFORD, *a Jamaican, was an official in the Brooklyn, New York branch of Garvey's UNIA. He was interviewed in Brooklyn in 1975.*

I was born August 26, 1898 in Manchester, Jamaica. My parents were Antoinette and Charles Crawford. My father was a mason and my mother a housewife. I went to a school run by the Presbyterian Church. I left Jamaica for the United States in 1924, when I was 26 years old.

I learned of Mr. Garvey when I was in Cuba in 1918. I had a sister there who told me about the UNIA branch in Cuba, and about Mr. Garvey and the work he was doing. The people in Cuba were proud that a Black man had come on the scene to work with them and to save them. I joined the organization in Cuba, then from Cuba I went back to Jamaica. I visited the branch in Kingston and was there when Mr. Garvey came to speak.

I was already a Garveyite when I arrived in the United States. I first read the Negro World in Jamaica. I was taken to Liberty Hall⁰ and I immediately joined. Garvey was in Kingston in 1923 or 1924, and he was holding several public meetings. I shook hands with him and he was very proud to meet us. Mr. Garvey came to Kingston on the Black Star Line. That was a sight to see. He was like a messiah to the people in Jamaica, where he had grown up. The meetings were held in the Ward Theater, and it was the biggest crowd we ever had in Kingston at that time. There were more people outside of the theater than in. I was proud of what he was doing. He was working to help save the race and redeem Africa. Meeting Mr. Garvey was like meeting a king.

When he spoke at the theater that night, he told people about their homeland in Africa and that he wanted to bring Black people's minds back to Africa, to make them Africa conscious. Mr. Garvey had no intention that all Black people would go back to Africa. But he did want to wake up the consciousness of Black people, to make them know from whence they came, the home of their ancestors.

I remember at one of Mr. Garvey's public meetings in Jamaica, he told them, "You say England is your mother country." He said, "Now if any of you here have a mother in England, hold up your hand," and when nobody did, he explained that England was the mother country of Jamaica, but not our mother country. "Your mother country is Africa." Mr. Garvey was a teacher.

I followed Mr. Garvey because he was able to tell us that it was not our color, it was our mind we had to use to get ahead in this world. You had to organize. His main objective was to organize Black people, teach Black people to be true to themselves and not to expect other people to do it for them. Mr. Garvey was a born leader, a diplomat, a dynamic speaker and whether you liked him or not, you had to listen to him and agree with what he had to say.

–Abridged from: Jeannette Smith-Irvin, *Marcus Garvey's Footsoldiers of the Universal Negro Improvement Association* (Africa World Press, 1989).

ELFREDA DUGLAS, *a Jamaican, remembers how Garvey fought to improve the lot of the island's working people. After forming a political party and labor union, Garvey sought election to the Jamaican legislative council in 1929. During the campaign, he called for unfair judges to be impeached; he was then arrested and jailed. Mrs. Duglas was interviewed in Jamaica in 1978.*

In 1925, only the top class could vote; poor people could not vote. They call the small man, poor man "masses," and the big man, you know, they call them "classes." Small man was not voting at all. The only people who used to get 10 shillings⁰ a week is the women what work up at King's House. When them work at King's House them get 10 shillings as washerwomen per week. Nobody else.

Now everything that Garvey say in 1925 now coming to pass. Him put out a manifesto. It was a Tuesday night, the 10th of September and him used these words: "A minimum wage for the working class of this country. Five days work, 8 hours a day you work and you work from Monday to Friday, and enough to get your pay on Saturday for when you go to the market." And him talk about agriculture: "You must plant food and feed yourselves." And irrigation. And him said, "Maternity leave with pay." And him say that, "If you send me to the council I and my colleagues will form a law that any judge or big men commit a crime in this country, them must be impeached and appear in court and sent on to prison as an ordinary criminal. And the criminal that is not satisfied with his trial can appeal."

That was a Tuesday night, and on Thursday they send police with summons on charges of seditious libel.° And when the case was tried, the judge fine him in circuit court 100 pounds° and three months in St. Catherine's district prison.

–Abridged from: *Jamaica: Caribbean Challenge* (EPICA, 1979).

RUTH SMITH, *an African-American, was driver and companion to Madame DeMena, an international organizer in the UNIA. She was interviewed in Detroit in 1987.*

I was born in Gadsen, Alabama, July 19, 1909. My parents were Homer and Ella Adkins Smith. There were eight children in my family, four boys and four girls. I was what they called the "knee baby," next to the baby. My family moved to Detroit and my early education was in the Detroit public schools.

I first came into contact with the UNIA in 1920 or 1921. My mother carried all of the girls into the UNIA so I was a member at a very young age. I grew up in the organization. Instead of going to church on Sunday, we would get up early and go to the Detroit division of the UNIA, diligently every Sunday.

The UNIA people would gather and the hall would be crowded every Sunday and we had a time. In the halls they would be selling papers and pop. When the main speaker came in, everyone would stand and then sit down. I was a member up until I got married. The man I married was a member of the UNIA. All of my social activities were in the UNIA—my life, my ideas revolved around the organization.

We used to have parades when I was a youngster in the Detroit division, and we participated with the city in general. We used to celebrate the eleventh of November, which was Armistice Day—the legions, Motor Corps, Black Cross Nurses, all of us, even the other divisions would come together sometimes on November 11th to celebrate.

Originally I was in the Women's Motor Corps. Madame DeMena was an international organizer, and her duties were to go to different places and organize divisions. I was her driver, her secretary, everything but Madame DeMena, but I was a good substitute. She was a small woman, but she had more power, she could really talk. I had a little old Plymouth. It would run awhile and get hot, and I would have to put water in it and so forth. We traveled from Chicago to the east coast.

I never regretted joining the UNIA. What was I going to do without the UNIA? What can you do without it? ... We do need now, as we needed then, the UNIA.

–Abridged from: Jeannette Smith-Irvin, *Marcus Garvey's Footsoldiers of the Universal Negro Improvement Association* (Africa World Press, 1989).

Vocabulary:

Liberty Hall: Harlem, New York headquarters of the UNIA

shilling: unit of British currency

seditious libel: statements aimed at overthrowing the government

pound: unit of British currency

READING

Burying Miss 'Mando

BY MICHAEL THELWELL

It was among ordinary working women and men, in the Caribbean and the United States, that Garvey's dream took hold.

The movie The Harder They Come, *starring musician Jimmy Cliff, told the fictional story of Ivan Martin, a Jamaican country boy who migrates to Kingston and becomes a notorious gunman and reggae star. With the film as inspiration, Jamaican novelist Michael Thelwell wrote* The Harder They Come, *taking us deeper into Ivan's story. As the book begins, young Ivan, about 12 years old, is living with his grandmother, Miss 'Mando, in the country. The village is close-knit and tradition-bound, and Ivan is secure in the warmth of family and community. But then his grandmother dies, and Ivan strikes out on his own for Kingston, the capital.*

In this passage from the book, villagers come together for the wake and funeral of Ivan's grandmother. The wake, also called "dinkyminny" or "set-up," is an important Jamaican tradition with roots in West Africa. After a person dies, friends and neighbors gather to cheer up the bereaved family. They spend the night singing and dancing, playing games and telling riddles and stories. Some wakes continue for nine nights, with ceremonies on the last night to symbolically assist the dead person's passage to the spirit world.

Maas' (Master) Nattie, a respected village leader, arranges for Miss 'Mando's funeral to follow tradition, "in the old way as according to the elders." *But one difference stands out: the emotional tribute to Marcus Garvey's Universal Negro Improvement Association, of which Miss 'Mando was a loyal member. Although the story takes place in 1950, several decades after Garvey's movement had peaked, it reflects the lasting impact Garvey had on people in Jamaica and throughout the Caribbean.*

Soon in the morning, before the sun had burned the dew from the grass, they came in numbers. Mostly women at first, in twos and threes—old friends and church sisters of the dead woman—wearing death sullen countenances, dirge-hymns° of mourning not far from their lips, asking almost challengingly after the manner of her going, listening carefully to the story, noting the exact position in which she was found, what she was wearing, what she had in her hand, regretting the absence of any "dying words," but nodding and exclaiming over the torn Bible, and then finally nodding judiciously as if to express their satisfaction with the account before going in to "take their leave," quite as if Miss 'Mando would be sitting up in bed to receive them.

On arrival, each new group waited until a number sufficient for another telling of the story was gathered, then they went to take their leave. No one entered the house before hearing of the manner of the death. The women took over the house and kitchen while Maas' Nattie spoke to the men.

In the house the close friends and distant kin of Miss 'Mando washed and anointed the body, dressed it and laid it out on the cooling board. They moved the deathbed outside the house to "fool the duppi°," built fires and went for water and firewood. The "dead water" that washed the body was carefully collected and this was brought and thrown at a certain place in the yard. Thereafter people were careful not to step on that spot. Maas' Nattie explained to a group of the older men that in accordance with Miss 'Mando's last wishes, "Everah t'ing gwine to be in de ol' way as 'cording to the elders. As it was with de ol' time people dem."

Ivan was sent to catch up two goats and a hog which were quickly butchered and hung to drain by a group under the direction of Joe Beck, who butchered and sold meat in the district. Small children accompanying their mothers were set to chase and catch the chickens scratching round in the underbrush. The men constructed a large arborlike shelter, a palm frond roof° raised on posts, beneath which the body would lie until burial and where the singing meeting and wake would be held at night. One group dug a pit over which the hog would be roasted, while others dug the grave next to the old graves down by the stone wall.

A cart was sent into Blue Bay to pick up the coffin, the arrival of which brought all work to a stop as the rich polished wood, the blue satin lining, and the brass handles gleaming like gold were admired and exclaimed over. Maas' Nattie beamed and nodded every time he heard someone saying that never before had a coffin so fine been seen in the district.

People continued to arrive, those coming from farther away who were not as close to the dead woman. Wishing to pay their respects, they all took some small part, if only symbolically, in the work. Most brought some contribution: a chicken, or some yams⁰ or bananas fresh from the field. Everything went into the pot. Soon the cooking spilled out of the kitchen and fires were built in the yard. Children were kept busy running home to bring pots or fetching pails of water from the standpipe⁰. Miss 'Mando's piety, industry, and decency, and that of her family was praised repeatedly, the praise growing more lavish with each speaker.

When the coffin was brought out and placed on the stand and the candles set at the head and feet, Maas' Nattie, in a departure from tradition, substituted a red, green, and black⁰ cloth for the usual white one, and the "set up⁰" or "singing meeting"

began. Drawn-out melancholy notes of long-meter sorrow songs hung over the mountains and valleys like a rich velvet shroud textured by passion. There were tales, mostly of death or about the character and deeds of the departed and her family. But there were also riddles, word games, duppi stories⁰, and much eating and drinking.

People, moved as much by the white rum and singing as by their remembrance of the dead, rose choked or even weeping to testify to their special relationship to Miss 'Mando. However, even with the frequent and dramatic outbursts of tears and wailing it could not really be said to be a sad occasion.

The first pale streaks had begun to show over Jancrow mountain and roosters were crowing to each other across the valley when Maas' Nattie announced that the burying would be at noon. Soon the only people left were stalwart and tireless ladies, laboring over fires on which was cooking food for the funeral feast, later that day.

The sun was almost directly overhead and the people had reassembled; there were more of them now as folks came from distant villages to be present at the burying. Miss 'Mando's sisters in the pocomania⁰ band were in full regalia: dazzling white robes stiff with starch and the peaked turbans which were the emblems of their sect. Maas' Nattie, resplendent in this year's burying suit made even more impressive by the red, green,

and black sash with the letters UNIA embroidered in black, was ready to give the command for the pallbearers to pick up their burden. He had earlier spent a lot of time in earnest discussion with four old people whom Ivan had never seen before, three men and a woman all dressed in rusty black, who had suddenly appeared on foot. They seemed tired as though they had come a long way. There was something formal, almost military about them and they were especially interesting to Ivan because of the shiny brass instruments they carried. They were introduced by Maas' Nattie as "You granny loyal comrade dem⁰" and Ivan wondered what unknown part of Miss 'Mando's life they represented. But Maas' Nattie wouldn't explain more than "You wi' see, bwai⁰, you wi' see."

Under a broiling sun, they carried the old lady in stately procession three times around the small yard, past the pig sty and the goat pen, over the low stone wall and through the coffee walk, to the new grave beside her husband's. The old-comrade woman beat a muffled drum roll on her Salvation Army drum and Mother Anderson and her pocomania sisters hummed slowly the tune of the lugubrious funeral standby:

Sleep on, sleep on
Sleep on an' take thy rest.
We loved thee true,
But Jesus love thee best
Good-bye ... good-bye ... good-bye.

It was hot by the graveside. Even the shade of the huge tree gave little relief. They set the

No. 21490

Shares One

INCORPORATED UNDER THE LAWS OF THE STATE OF DELAWARE

BLACK STAR LINE, INC.

CAPITAL STOCK $10,000,000
SHARES $5. EACH

This Certifies that *Theresa Moore* is the owner of *One Share of the Capital Stock of*

BLACK STAR LINE, INC. full paid and non-assessable

transferable only on the books of this Corporation in person or by Attorney upon surrender of this Certificate properly endorsed.

IN WITNESS WHEREOF, the said Corporation has caused this Certificate to be signed by its duly authorized officers and its Corporate Seal to be hereunto affixed this ___ day of ___ A.D. 19__

Secretary-Treasurer

President

A $5 *share in The Black Star Line*

coffin down and looked to Maas' Nattie. He held up his hands in a priestly gesture as though asking for silence, even though the only sound was a few stifled sobs from the sisters.

"You all know dat our dear departed sister was very dear to mi soul—to all a we."

"Ahmen."

"Praise Gawd."

"Before she go, she leave me wid two las' wish. She say dat she want a big funeral, an' praise be to Gawd an' the love and respeck of all of unu[0] she have dat. ' He looked at the gathering approvingly.

"Ahmen. Praise His Holy name."

"Den she say she want to bury in the spirit. An' you can see dat. All a' unu is witnesses to dat."

"Hallelulah!"

"But next to her Gawd and her people dem, de t'ing that was mos' precious to her was the vision an' inspiration of the honorable Marcus Mosiah Garvey, the Leader an' Redeemer of de People." Maas' Nattie spaced each syllable of the name out like an exhortation. On the word "Garvey" the four old people pulled themselves smartly to attention and the old woman whispered fervently,

"Allelujah!"

"Many of unu will be too young to know dis," Maas' Nattie went on, "but the woman you burying was one of the *staunches'* and mos' *steadfast* and *earlies'* members of the Universal Negro Improvement Association in these parts."

Again a stiffening among the four ancients and murmurs of agreement.

"So Miss 'Mando's, res' her

soul, las' wish was to bury like a soldier of the Lawd and of Garvey." He stretched out his hand and the old woman marched forward and handed him a cloth somewhat smaller than the one he had draped over the coffin during the wake. It had embroidered on it in shaky gold lettering AMANDA MARTIN 1880-1950, and in smaller letters *Rise up ye mighty race*. Maas' Nattie exhibited it proudly so all could see. There were approving cries from the crowd as they read the inscription. He reverently draped it over the coffin, saying something that no one could hear. Then he drew himself up, faced the people, and in a voice throbbing with feeling and heroic fervor he declaimed:

> *Ethiopia dou land of our fathers⁰,*
>
> *Dou land where the Gods love to be,*
>
> *As de storm clouds at night suddenly gadders,*
>
> *Our armies come rushing to dee.*
>
> *We must in de fight be victorious*
>
> *Our swords are outthrust to gleam*
>
> *For us will victory be glorious*
>
> *When led by de red, black and green.*

Here, the four rickety remnants of a dispersed army raised their reedy old voices in the passionate litany to a dead leader, a scattered movement, and a dream deferred but not forgotten:

> *Advance, advance to victory*
>
> *Let Africa's power be seen!*
>
> *Advance, advance to victory,*
>
> *With de might of de Red, Black and Green!*

The thin and ancient voices swelled with affirmation and a wistful grandeur on the last lines. Then, after a suitable pause, the men raised their instruments, the brass gleaming like dull gold in a shaft of sunlight. They stood there, Miss 'Mando's guard of honor, trembling right hands holding the brass to toothless lips, left fists clenched over their hearts. For reasons that he didn't understand Ivan felt a rush of hot tears behind his eyes. The old lady began a steady, low beat in a military cadence. The trombone missed the beat and started first with a windy wheeze, not unlike someone breaking wind, but quickly recovered and the brassy notes of the anthem quavered out, tentatively and discordant at first, then filling the valley with a broken grandeur that was all the more stirring. When the echoes of the last note died away, they buried Miss 'Mando.

–Abridged from: Michael Thelwell, *The Harder They Come* (Grove Press, 1980)

Vocabulary

dirge-hymns: funeral hymns

duppi (or duppy): ghost or spirit of a dead person

palm frond roof: temporary roof woven from the fibers of the coconut palm

yam: starchy root vegetable

standpipe: outdoor water faucet

red, green and black: colors of the UNIA

set-up: first night of a wake

duppi stories: ghost stories

pocomania: Jamaican cult mixing Christian fundamentalism with African religious customs

dem: them (indicates plural)

bwai: boy

unu (or oonoo): you, plural (originally from the Twi language)

Ethiopia thou land of our fathers ...: anthem of Garvey's UNIA

Certificate of membership in the UNIA

UNIT FOUR: Louise Bennett, National Poetess of Jamaica
TEACHER GUIDE

▶ **OBJECTIVES**

Students will:

1. Explain Louise Bennett's contribution to Jamaican culture and why it is important

2. Define Jamaican patois, its relationship to English and its role in Jamaican culture

3. Discuss the social implications of dominant versus vernacular languages

▶ **QUESTIONS FOR DISCUSSION**

1. What is the official language of Jamaica? What language do most people speak? How are they different?

2. Which is superior—patois or English? How did you decide? What is the purpose of language? Can one language be superior to another? Why or why not?

3. Miss Lou says that Jamaicans have more to say in their own language than in English. Is the language you speak at home different from the one you speak in class? If it is, are there things you can say better in your home language?

4. "The people 'Miss Lou' loved were different from the person she was being schooled to become." Explain.

5. In the poem "Back to Africa," how does the person addressing Miss Matty feel about going back to Africa? Why?

6. In the poem "Dutty Tough," what items are named as having gone up in price? Why are these things important?

7. "Rain a-fall but dutty tough" [the rain is falling but the ground is tough] is a Jamaican proverb. What do you think it means?

8. Why did Louise Bennett call her poem about migration to Britain "Colonization in Reverse?"

▶ **SUGGESTED ACTIVITIES**

1. For the flavor of Jamaican patois, play Jamaican folk songs and children's games sung by Louise Bennett, available on record (see Resources).

2. If there are any Jamaican students in the class, ask them to read Bennett's poems aloud. Otherwise, ask students to read the poems silently. Next, have students "translate" the poems into standard English, a line at a time. The English versions supplied with the poems are for the instructor's use in this exercise; they should not be handed out to students. Finally, lead a discus-

sion of the poems' meanings.

3. This unit can be used to lead into a larger discussion of dominant versus popular languages. American English is the dominant language in the United States; students may speak another language or dialect at home, such as Black English. Which language do they feel most comfortable in? In which situations is one or the other language more appropriate? What are some advantages and disadvantages of speaking two languages or dialects?

Encourage students to play music (such as rap) or read aloud poetry or stories which use their vernacular language. Discuss the function language plays in these artistic expressions. How does it help convey the artist's message?

▶ **RESOURCES**

1. Books of Louise Bennett's poetry include *Jamaica Labrish* (Sangster's, 1966) and *Selected Poems* (Sangster's, 1982). There is also a collection of her Anansi stories, *Anancy and Miss Lou* (Sangster's, 1979). Available from Caribbean Books.

2. Louise Bennett sings on *Jamaican Folk Songs* (album no. FW6846) and *Children's Jamaican Songs and Games* (album no. FC7250). Available from Smithsonian Folkway Records, 416 Hungerford Drive, Suite 320, Rockville, MD 20850. (301) 443-2314.

3. Paula Burnett, ed., *The Penguin Book of Caribbean Verse in English* (Penguin Books, 1986). Includes folk rhymes, poems in patois, dub poetry, calypso and reggae songs.

INTRODUCTION

Louise Bennett, National Poetess of Jamaica

The Europeans who colonized the Caribbean used their own languages as the standard of communication in their colonies. As a result of this colonial past, Caribbean people today speak Spanish, English, French and Dutch. These are the "official" languages of the region, used for government, education and public life.

But these are not the languages most Caribbean people use in daily life. Instead, they speak what are known as Creole languages. These developed during the colonial era, when Africans of many different language groups arrived in the Caribbean. To communicate, they had to create a common tongue. Gradually new languages emerged, blending elements of African and European languages together into new forms.

The Creole language spoken in Jamaica is called patois (pronounced "patwa"). It is also sometimes called "dialect." Patois draws most of its vocabulary from English, but African languages influenced the grammar and contributed some words (see Unit 2). Jamaicans learn English in school, and those with more formal education speak both English and patois fluently. The majority of Jamaicans, however, express themselves most fluently in patois.

Although millions of Caribbean people speak Creole languages, the colonial system defined these languages as inferior, and for a long time many people accepted this view. Standard English remains the only accepted means of public communication in Jamaica; it is used for newspapers and television, schools, government offices and courts of law. As a result, patois-speaking Jamaicans are at a disadvantage in making their voices heard.

One person who has worked to change this is folk artist Louise Bennett. She is an educated Jamaican who has never forgotten her roots, and who believes that Jamaicans can best express how they think and feel in their own language. She was the first to write and perform poetry in patois for a national audience. Her popularity helped change negative attitudes about patois. Nesha Z. Haniff, a Guyanese writer, profiles Louise Bennett in "Miss Lou."

Bennett's poem "Colonization in Reverse" comments humorously on the mass migration of Jamaicans to Britain during the 1950s. "Dutty Tough" captures the desperation of the average Jamaican faced with rising prices and hard times. In "Back to Africa," Bennett suggests the skepticism many Jamaicans felt toward the Rastafarians' back-to-Africa movement, and their acceptance of a Jamaican national identity.

Louise Bennett ("Miss Lou")

READING
Miss Lou

BY NESHA Z. HANIFF

Meme, her grandmother, called her "Bibs"; everyone in Jamaica calls her "Miss Lou"; her name is Louise Bennett. She was born in Kingston, Jamaica, on the seventh day of September, 1919.

She was an extroverted child who had a quick mind, an ear for sounds and a knack for recitation and performance. These qualities made her popular. She was always making up stories on the teacher, coining phrases, poems, songs and rhymes.

As a child, she wrestled with the double messages around her. The people she loved, and who loved her, had dinkyminnies[0], sang folk songs, had wakes, and pocomanias[0] and spoke in dialect[0.] Yet at school you were supposed to recite English poems, speak "correctly" and write with "proper" grammar. The people she loved were different from the person she was being schooled to become. This was not true just for herself, but true for all the other children.

When she began to create her dialect poems and recite them, she was in an unconscious way legitimizing herself and her friends. They listened to her not only because she was creative, funny, and a good performer, but because in expressing the humor, beauty and love around her, she was speaking out not only for herself, but for them too. She spoke what they knew and understood. What was Jamaican and black also belonged on center stage.

When I used to go to school the folklore was very strong. You would hear people singing the folksong on the streets. The first time I heard a whole lot of them was when Meme died at the Dinky-minny. Dinkyminny is a function that they have to cheer up the family of a dead person. They would sing and dance. A lot of families don't allow "Dinky" in their yard, because, you see, anything black was bad.

Miss Lou's ambition was always to write. At first she wrote poems, but they were in standard English, not in the dialect form for which she is now famous. Her first dialect poem was written when she was fourteen years old.

I was in high school and I was going to what we call "movies theater" and you paid nine pence and you went to matinee. So now any day we come home from school early and we have matinee money, we could dress up in we clothes and we go pon tram car and we go to Crossroads. Well my dear one day I was dressed and waiting on a tram car. This car was a market tram, it wasn't really a market car. The market people sat at the back with their baskets, so they cannot sit in front, so they are very annoyed when anybody come and sit in the back—that is anybody who is not a market person. When I was on the tram that day, there were no seats in front, so I decided to go in the back. Well I was fourteen and portly and was dressed up so I didn't look like a fourteen-year-old. So one woman said to another woman, "Pread out youself, one dress woman[0] a come. Pread out." And me dear everybody start pread dem apron all over de seat dem. And I wrote the first set on this, when I went home I wrote it. The next day I tried it out in school and it sweet them[0.]

This was the start of her writing career, but most importantly, she began to write material which she herself performed. They were always based on her own experiences, things she observed or heard.

Then I started to write and I realized more and more that this is what I should do because this is what I understand and this is what the people were saying. More was being said in [patois] than in any other thing and nobody was listening ...

Of course we must learn English but I think that Jamaican people have more to say in their language than in English. It is the language of the country. It is three hundred years we been talking it. It is not a corruption of anything. It is, mind you, a regional dialect because it belongs to an island, we can't expect everybody to understand it. After all English only start 'pon a little island over there and we still learn it.

She became Miss Lou, a national figure. As the popularity of her work grew, she became conscious of the legitimacy and importance of what she was doing. She started to study the Jamaican dialect in earnest and to gather stories and sayings and other expressions of the folk culture. She was constantly being invited to village festivals where people not only recited her poetry, but performed and interpreted her poems. She started a movement that took on a life of its own.

Louise Bennett's life has been full of awards, from a little book of Claude McKay's[0] poems given to her by Miss Biggs in school, to the Musgrave Gold Medal of Jamaica. The awards, the books, the poems, the articles are too numerous to mention. She has appeared on film, been written about, talked about and interviewed. She has taught and performed in England and in the Caribbean. 1986 marked her 50th year as a performer, an event celebrated in Gordon Town, her home, and in England and North America.

Her eyes reflect the light and laughter that her artistry evokes. She has seen the Jamaica that she knew and loved at first disparaged and then take center stage. Now the beauty and integrity in the language and culture of the Jamaican people is a force because Louise Bennett was among the first to stand up for it.

–Abridged from: Nesha Z. Haniff, *Blaze A Fire: Significant Contributions of Caribbean Women* (Sister Vision: Black Women and Women of Colour Press, 1988).

Vocabulary

dinkyminny: first night of a traditional Jamaican wake (also called "set-up")

pocomanias: pocomania ceremonies. Pocomania is a Jamaican cult mixing Christian fundamentalism with African religious customs. Worship combines Bible reading and prayer with singing, dancing, drumming and spirit possession.

dialect: Jamaican patois

dress woman: well-dressed woman, i.e. not a market woman

it sweet them: it appealed to them

Claude McKay: well-known Jamaican novelist and poet

READING
Poems by Louise Bennett

"COLONIZATION IN REVERSE"

Wat a joyful news, Miss Mattie,
I feel like me heart gwine burs
Jamaica people colonizin
Englan in reverse.
By de hundred, by de tousan
From country and from town,
By de ship-load, by de plane-load
Jamaica is Englan boun.
Dem a-pour out a Jamaica,
Everybody future plan
Is fe get a big-time job
An settle in de mother lan⁰˙
What a islan! What a people!
Man an woman, old an young
Just a-pack dem bag an baggage
An tun history upside dung!

Vocabulary
mother lan: motherland, i.e. the colonial power, Britain

"BACK TO AFRICA"

Back to Africa Miss Matty?
Yuh noh know wha yuh dah-sey?
Yuh haffe come from some weh fus,
Before yuh go back deh?
Me know sey dat yuh great great great
Gramma was African,
But Matty, doan yuh great great great
Grampa was Englishman?
Den yuh great granmada fada
By yuh fada side was Jew?
An yuh grampa by yuh mada side
Was Frenchie parley-vous!
But de balance o' yuh family
Yuh whole generation
Oonoo⁰ all bawn dung a Bun Grung⁰
Oonoo all is Jamaican!
Den is weh yuh gwine Miss Matty?
Oh, you view de countenance⁰,

An between yuh an de Africans
Is great resemblance!
Ascorden to dat, all dem blue-y'eye
Wite American,
Who-fa great grandpa was Englishman
Mus go back a Englan!
Wat a debil of a bump-an-bore⁰,
Rig-jig⁰ an palam-pam⁰!
Ef de whole worl' start fe go back
Weh dem great grandpa come from!
Ef a hard time yuh dah-run from
Teck yuh chance, but Matty, do
Sure o' weh yuh come from so yuh got
Somewhere fe come-back to!
Go a foreign⁰, seek yuh fortune,
But noh tell nobody sey
Yuh dah-go fe seek yuh homelan
For a right deh so yuh deh!

Vocabulary
oonoo (or unu): you, plural
Bun Grung: Burned Ground (a place)
countenance: face
bump-an-bore: pushing and jostling
rig-jig: lively, crowded dance
palam-pam: noise and confusion
go a foreign: travel abroad

"DUTTY TOUGH"

Sun a-shine but tings noh bright
Doah pot a-bwile⁰, bickle⁰ noh nuff
River flood but wata scarce, yah
Rain a-fall but dutty tuff⁰!
Tings so bad, dat now-a-days wen
Yuh ask smaddy⁰ how dem do
Dem fraid yuh tek it tell dem back
So dem noh answer yuh!
Noh care omuch we dah-work fa
Hard-time still eena we shu't⁰
We dah-fight, Hard-Time a-beat we

Dem might raise we wages, but
One poun[0] gawn up pon we pay, an
We noh feel noh merriment
For ten poun gawn up pon we food
An ten poun pon we rent!
Saltfish[0] gawn up! Mackeral[0] gawn up!
Pork an beef gawn up same way
An wan rice and butter ready
Dem jus go pon holiday[0]!
Cloth, boot, pin an needle gawn up
Ice, bread, taxes, wata-rate!

Kersene ile, gasoline, gawn up
An de pound devaluate[0]!
Sun a-shine an pot a-bwile, but
Tings noh bright, bickle noh nuff!
Rain a-fall, river dah-flood, but
Wata scarce an dutty tuff!

Vocabulary

bwile: boil

bickle: food

rain a-fall but dutty tough: Rain falls but the dirt is tough. A proverb.

smaddy: somebody

shu't: shirt

poun: pound (Jamaica was still a British colony when the poem was written, and the pound was legal currency.)

saltfish: fish (usually cod) preserved by drying and salting. A staple of the Jamaican diet.

mackeral: canned fish, like sardines

holiday: vacation

de pound devaluate: The pound has been devaluated, i.e. is worth less than before.

–Reprinted from: Louise Bennett, *Jamaica Labrish* (Sangster's Book Stores, 1966).

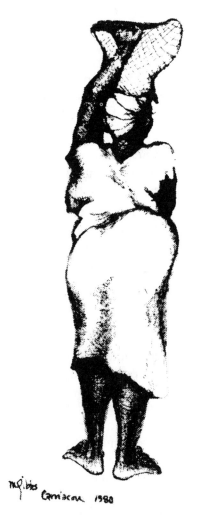

Artist: *Michelle Gibbs*

KEY TO POEMS IN PATOIS

Colonization in Reverse

What a joyful news, Miss Mattie
I feel like my heart will burst
Jamaican people colonizing
England in reverse

By the hundred, by the thousand
From country and from town
By the ship-load, by the plane-load
Jamaica is England-bound

They pour out of Jamaica
Everybody's future plan
Is to get a big-time job
And settle in the motherland

What an island! What a people!
Man and woman, old and young
Just pack their bags and baggage
And turn history upside down!

Back to Africa

Back to Africa, Miss Matty?
You don't know what you're saying?
You have to come from somewhere first
Before you go back there?

I know that your great-great-great
Grandma was African
But Matty, wasn't your great-great-great
Grandpa an Englishman ?

Then your great-grandmother's father
On your father's side was Jewish?
And your grandpa on your mother's side
Was "Frenchie parlez-vous"!

But the balance of your family
Your whole generation
You were all born down at Burned Ground
You are all Jamaican!

Then where are you going, Miss Matty?
Oh, you view the countenance
And between you and the Africans
Is a great resemblance!

According to that, all those blue-eyed
White Americans
Whose great-grandfathers were English
Must go back to England!

What a devil of a bump-a-bore
Rig-jig and palam-pam
If the whole world starts to go back

Where their great-grandpa came from!
If it's hard times you're running from
Take your chance, but Matty, do
Be sure of where you've come from so you've got
Somewhere to come back to!

Go to foreign lands, seek your fortune
But don't say to anyone
That you're going to seek your homeland
Because you're already right there!

Dutty Tough

The sun is shining, but things aren't bright
Though the pot is boiling, the food's not enough
The river floods but the water is scarce, yeah
Rain falls but the ground is tough

Things are so bad, that nowadays when
You ask somebody how they're doing
They're afraid you'll take it and tell them back
So they don't answer you

It doesn't matter how much we work
Hard times are still "in our shirt"
We fight, but hard times are beating us
They might raise our wages, but ...

Our pay goes up by one pound, and
We feel no merriment
For our food costs go up by ten pounds
And ten pounds on our rent

Saltfish gone up! Mackeral gone up!
Pork and beef gone up the same way
And when rice and butter are ready
They just go on holiday [vacation, i.e. disappear]

Cloth, boots, pins and needles gone up
Ice, bread, taxes, water rate
Kerosene oil, gasoline, gone up
And the pound has been devaluated

The sun is shining, and the pot is boiling, but
Things aren't bright, the food's not enough
Rain is falling, the river floods, but
Water's scarce and the ground is tough

UNIT FIVE: In the Country
TEACHER GUIDE

▶ **OBJECTIVES**

Students will:

1. Learn about crops grown in Jamaica
2. Analyze the role higglers play in the Jamaican economy
3. Appreciate the independence and pride of the small farmer

▶ **QUESTIONS FOR DISCUSSION**

1. What is a higgler? Why are they important to the Jamaican economy?

2. What are some of the advantages and disadvantages of higgling as a means of making a living? Consider: earnings, job security, independence and freedom, working conditions, risks for the future. Support your points with examples from Miss Tiny's story.

3. Which of the foods eaten in Jamaica do you eat frequently? Have you ever seen these crops growing? Which Jamaican fruits and vegetables have you never seen or tasted?

5. In "Song of the Banana Man," how does the farmer feel about his life? Why?

▶ **SUGGESTED ACTIVITIES**

1. [Middle school students] Ask students to pretend they are Miss Tiny. Her van has just been stolen and she must decide what to do. Each student writes two paragraphs explaining her/his feelings, thoughts and plans.

2. The class visits a grocery store, preferably one catering to a Caribbean or Latin American clientele. Look for the fruits and vegetables mentioned in the readings. If possible, purchase samples for tasting, such as coconuts, mangoes and papayas. If there are Caribbean students in the class, they may want to share recipes using the foods or demonstrate preparation of simple dishes.

▶ **RESOURCES**

1. Pat Ellis, ed., *Women of the Caribbean* (Zed Press, 1987). Essays by Caribbean women writers on women and work, the family, education, culture and development. Includes a chapter on higgling. Available from Zed Books.

INTRODUCTION
In the Country

For more than 400 years, the Jamaican economy revolved around one product: sugar. Almost all of colonial Jamaica's flat, fertile land was controlled by English planters. Except for a brief time around 1900 when the banana trade boomed, "King Sugar" dominated Jamaica's economy until the 1950s.

In 1952, North American companies began mining Jamaican bauxite, and the mineral ore replaced sugar as the island's chief export. The Jamaican government also worked to develop tourism, manufacturing and other industries. By 1986, tourism was Jamaica's largest earner of foreign exchange.

A Farming Nation

The new industries brought income into Jamaica and provided some jobs, but most people continued to make their living from the land. Today, agriculture is the country's largest employer, accounting for more than one-third of the workforce. Sixty percent of Jamaicans live in the rural areas of the island—"in the country."

Many of them are small farmers, owners of less than five acres of land. The small farming tradition began when slaves tended gardens of their own to add to their food rations and earn money. After emancipation,

Artist: *Vernal Reuben*

many former slaves became independent farmers, growing and trading a wide variety of crops.

Land ownership became synonymous with freedom. Even today, there is a strong feeling among many Jamaicans that only when you own "your own piece of ground" are you truly independent and secure. This pride is expressed in Evan Jones' much-loved poem, "Song of the Banana Man."

Jamaican small farmers—many of them women—survive on very little land and plenty of hard work. Much of their land is mountainous and hard to cultivate; larger landowners control most of the best flat lands. Despite these handicaps, small farmers grow most of the fruits and vegetables consumed in Jamaica.

Another important group are traders, usually women, who are known as "higglers." They purchase produce from the farmers and sell it in country and city markets, which may be in the open air or in a large, roofed building. Each seller sits behind her piles of goods, calling customers to come and buy.

Higglers also sell other items people need, such as soap, razor blades, shoes, thread, safety pins and ballpoint pens. Like Miss Tiny, some even travel by boat or plane to other countries to bring back goods that are not easily available in Jamaica. These international higglers are an increasingly crucial element of the Jamaican economy.

The higgler is an independent businesswoman who must use careful planning to succeed. Miss Tiny was successful in part

Higgler and shopper in a Kingston market

because she saved her earnings and reinvested them in her business. Like many Caribbean women, she saves not by depositing money in a bank, but by joining a savings club. Each member pays a set amount per week into a common pool; each week it is a different member's turn to draw the total for her own use. Jamaicans call this method of saving "throwing partners."

The higgler is her own boss, and she enjoys a measure of economic independence and freedom that wage workers do not have. But as Miss Tiny's story shows, a higgler's life is by no means an easy one.

READING
Miss Tiny

BY NESHA Z. HANIFF

Miss Tiny is a higgler. Everyone calls her Miss Tiny, but her real name is Esmine Antoine and she was born on the l9th of August, 1935 in St. Andrew, Jamaica.

At the time she was growing up in Jamaica, secondary school[0] was not free and so was a difficult thing for children of poor families to pursue. Leaving her three-month-old baby with her mother, she left for Kingston[0] at the age of sixteen armed with one dollar and dreams of making a living for herself.

I had a hard life, a very very hard life. From I have my six children, I don't get a hundred dollars from one of them father. Me one[0] have to shoulder dem burden.

In Kingston she stayed with a friend and bought some thyme, scallion and paper bags and sold them on a little tray on Princess Street. She was accustomed to selling as she had often helped her mother who sold produce in the St. Andrew market. This was her start as a higgler in Kingston.

In Jamaica, almost all higglers are women. The term "higgler" originally referred to a woman who bought items wholesale from "country people" and sold mainly agricultural produce. Today higgler is a general term for women who run small vendoring businesses.

Most women are initiated into the business by their mothers. The higgler sells her fare either on the streets or in open spaces in the market, so she must guard her "load" against theft. The guard is usually a child, in most cases, a daughter. Miss Tiny was the guard who kept an eye on the produce, who ran errands, helped her mother carry her bundles and who sold and interacted with customers. When she went to Kingston, selling was the only profession she knew; it influenced her start as a "tray girl."

She did this type of selling for five years. At the end of each week she would take the money she made and buy things for the baby and send them to her mother in St. Andrew.

Meanwhile, she met a man with whom she had four children. She heard that a little shop was for rent and decided to start a business of her own. She, the children's father and the children moved into the back of the shop. Miss Tiny ran a food shop, selling fried fish and ackee[0]. She was now twenty-one years old. However, the shop business soon ended because the owners wanted the premises for their own purposes.

The relationship with the children's father slowly disintegrated and she launched into a new phase of the vendoring business. She became a fishwoman. The small-scale fish vendors got their supplies from the large fishing boats that came into Kingston, and Miss Tiny, upon learning this, supplied herself with small quantities of fish from these boats. Buying large quantities of fish required refrigeration, which she did not have.

Slowly she began to increase the amount she could sell. She heard that it was cheaper to buy from fishermen in the country. This entailed leaving on a truck in the evening, waiting for the boats to come in, sleeping on the beach, making the purchase and leaving by five o'clock the next morning to catch the market business.

Miss Tiny saw that her life would be simplified by two things: her own transportation and refrigeration. Her first purchase was a freezer. This allowed her to buy large quantities and made the daily trip unnecessary. After a while she was able to buy her own van, which her son learned to drive.

To be a higgler with your own transportation is quite an impressive feat. Miss Tiny was able to realize this dream. Not only was she able to buy a freezer and a van, she was able to buy her own home and furnish it.

These acquisitions meant security and comfort for her family and herself, but they required accumulation of capital. It is difficult for higglers to save money as most of their money is reinvested in their business. Those who do, do so by "throwing partners." This is the informal savings system that is called "throwing box" in Guyana and "susu" in Trinidad. Miss Tiny was able to acquire her house, van, and equipment through this savings system.

In 1980, the van was stolen and her life as a fishwoman came to an abrupt end. She entered into a new phase of higglering. She became an international higgler, one of the hundreds of Caribbean women who travel to Puerto Rico, Panama, the Bahamas, the Cayman Islands and the Virgin Islands to buy and sell.

Miss Tiny's main territory was Panama. On her first trip she went with a friend who was already in the business and who had an intricate system of contacts. The scallion and rum and thyme brought from Jamaica would be sold to these contacts. In this way, the women would acquire the money for the next step: the purchase of items that were both needed and scarce in Jamaica.

Is we di higglers bring in things that people want and you can't get. We bring in elastic when you couldn't get it and razor blades and all dem kinda things. And now they say how higglers overcharge. Nobody know how hard we work and struggle to bring dem things in.

Higglering in Jamaica is an intricate and carefully built system of checks and balances. It is a female system which could not survive on money alone. Almost everything is done on trust. A woman must establish a credible reputation. Produce is sold to one woman who goes to market and then returns with payment. A woman must be careful not to alienate other higglers who buy from her wholesale, because she might lose a steady source of income. Similarly, those who buy must always try to pay, otherwise they may lose their source of supply and jeopardize their business.

Miss Tiny is now fifty-six years old. She has been a tray girl, a food shop owner, a fishwoman and is now a higgler dealing in international trade. She has many worries: dealing with customs officers, paying her bills, holding on to what she has. She worries about the injustice of losing her van and not having any hope of recovering it. What will happen to higglers and what could she do if she could not do higglering?

Miss Tiny's hand is slightly maimed. A few years ago a fish bone pierced her hand and it became infected. There are other marks on Miss Tiny's life and body that reflect the struggling times of a higgler. Her eyes are worn, her voice rasps because it has argued and agitated all her life and her life is like that of many other women in her business.

She went a little beyond the others by buying a van. To many, it may not seem like a significant act; to a higgler it signifies success. She became a model for other higglers to emulate.

Miss Tiny speaks for herself and for all higglers when she says:

I should get a medal every Heroes' Day° as a one woman. Every Heroes' Day I should get a gold medal to go through all these troubles and nobody don't give me a ting. Is me and me alone. Every Heroes' Day I should get a medal, for I struggle hard with my life and for my children I is a hero.

–Adapted from: Nesha Z. Haniff, *Blaze a Fire: Significant Contributions of Caribbean Women* (Sister Vision, 1988).

Vocabulary

secondary school: high school

Kingston: capital of Jamaica

me one: I alone

ackee: Fruit which grows on trees. When cooked, its light yellow flesh tastes like scrambled eggs.

Heroes' Day: national holiday honoring figures from Jamaican history

READING
On A Higgler's Table

Many of the foods grown and eaten in Jamaica are familiar to North Americans: carrots, eggplant, onions, corn, oranges, grapefruit, limes and many other foods we know. But have you ever tasted ackee and saltfish, roast breadfruit, or guava jam? Here are some of the food crops that one might find on a Jamaican higgler's table.

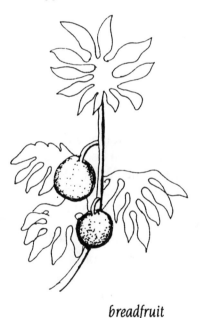

breadfruit

The **ACKEE** is Jamaica's national fruit. It originated in West Africa, where it is called by its Twi name, *ankye*. The red-and-yellow fruit grows on a tall tree. When ripe, the fruit splits to reveal shiny black seeds surrounded by yellow flesh; cooked, the flesh resembles scrambled eggs. Ackee cooked with dried salted fish ("saltfish") is the national dish of Jamaica.

BANANAS were once Jamaica's "green gold." The banana tree, actually a large herb, was introduced into the Caribbean by the Spanish. It became economically important to Jamaica in the late 1800s as sugar exports were declining. Bananas were grown by small farmers and marketed in the United States by large U.S. firms, notably the United Fruit Company. Boats transporting bananas between Jamaica and the United States also brought the first tourists to Jamaica. Today, Jamaica exports most of its bananas to England.

The **BREADFRUIT** tree, native to the Pacific islands, grows up to 70 feet tall. It bears a round green fruit about the size of a soccer ball. Boiled, roasted or fried breadfruit is a staple starch for many rural Jamaicans.

CALLALOO is a leafy green plant which many Jamaicans grow in their gardens. It is probably native to the Americas. The vitamin-rich leaves are cooked and eaten like spinach, or in soup.

COCOA is indigenous to the Americas. Columbus took some back to Europe with him on his return from the Caribbean. The cocoa tree bears pods which contain seeds called cocoa beans. The beans are dried, roasted and ground, then combined with sugar to make chocolate. High-quality Jamaican cocoa is grown for domestic consumption and export.

COCONUTS, the fruit of the coconut palm, have many uses. The white flesh of the mature coconut produces oil for cooking and making soap. Grated, it is used in baked goods and candies; or it is pressed to yield coconut milk, a creamy liquid used in cooking. Unripe coconuts are a popular item on roadside stands in Jamaica. The coconut vendor splits the nut, scooping out the young flesh or "jelly" for eating. The clear liquid from the center of the nut, called coconut water, is a refreshing beverage. The fronds of the coconut palm are woven into hats, mats and roofs.

COFFEE from the slopes of

coffee

Jamaica's Blue Mountains is internationally famous. Indigenous to Ethiopia, coffee was introduced to Jamaica by a former British governor of the island in 1728. It is a small tree which produces berries which turn bright red when ripe. Inside are the coffee "beans" which are roasted and ground to make coffee for drinking. Jamaica exports its high-quality coffee, especially to Japan.

GROUND PROVISIONS are the starchy root vegetables which form an important part of the Caribbean diet. There are many varieties, all of them the "tuber" or underground part of vine-like plants. Yams, the most important variety, were brought from Africa to the Caribbean. There

yams

are many different types of yam. Cassava is indigenous to the Americas and was a staple food of the Arawaks. It is also called manioc and yuca. Cassava is used to make the popular cassava bread, called "bammy." Other types of ground provisions eaten in Jamaica are sweet potatoes, cocos (also called

tannia or yautía), dasheen and badoo.

The **GUAVA** tree grows wild in Jamaica. Its name comes from

guava

the Arawak language. The tree bears a small round fruit with sweet flesh which is eaten raw or made into juice or jelly.

GUNGO PEAS are eaten in a favorite Jamaican dish, "rice and peas." They grow on a small shrub and are also called pigeon peas or congo peas.

MANGOES grow all over Jamaica and the Caribbean. The tall mango tree, which originated in India, bears an oval fruit which ripens from green to yellow or red. The sweet orange flesh is eaten fresh or made into juice, jelly or chutney. There are many varieties of mango.

The **NASEBERRY** is a short tree native to the Americas. It bears a brown, plum-sized fruit with black seeds and sweet, creamy flesh. Elsewhere naseberry is called sapodilla.

PAWPAW is the Jamaican name

for papaya. A short tree native to the Americas, pawpaw grows wild in Jamaica. The fruit has mild orange flesh surrounding a mass of dark jelly-like seeds. In

the Spanish-speaking Caribbean pawpaw is called *lechosa* or *fruta bomba*.

PIMENTO, known in the U.S. as "allspice," is indigenous to the Americas. It is a berry which combines the flavors of cinnamon, clove, pepper and nutmeg. It is one of Jamaica's minor exports.

SUGAR cane was once Jamaica's only export crop. The Spanish introduced cane into the Caribbean from the Canary Islands. During the colonial era, sugar grown on giant plantations was

pawpaw

the basis of the notorious sugar-slave trade. The market for Caribbean sugar declined in the 1800s, but most Caribbean countries, including Jamaica, still grow and export some sugar. Sugar cane is a tall, fibrous reed which can grow to a height of 15 feet. Many steps are necessary to extract the sweet juice and process it into white granulated sugar. Partially-refined dark sugar, called "wet sugar," is sold in Jamaican markets. One can also buy short lengths of cane for chewing as a snack.

The **TAMARIND** tree bears long brown pods with flat seeds and a sour pulp. The pulp is eaten fresh or made into juice, jelly or candy.

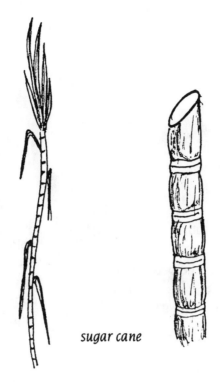

sugar cane

tamarind

Artist: Katherine Rawson

READING
Jamaica Alphabet

A CHILDREN'S SONG
BY LOUISE BENNETT

A is for ackee, saltfish'° best friend
B is for bammy°, banana and then
C is for cocoa, coconut, callaloo
D is for dumpling° and dokunu°
E is for egg, nourishing fe eat
F is for fufu° when yuh lose yuh teeth
G is for guava and gungo peas
H is for honey come straight from the bees
I is for injun cane° make you look strong and well
J is for jackfruit° don't judge by the smell
K is for kingfruit° big and juicy them grow
L is for lottus°, same stinkin-toe
M is for mango what a something sweet
N is for naseberry smoothness can't beat
O is for ochro° it slippery mi chile
P is for plantain° roasted or boiled
Q is for Quashie° him good stuff have charms
R, rice and peas°, Jamaican Coat of Arms
S is susumba° with saltfish and rice
T is tangerine, every peg° sweet and nice
U is for ugly° it taste good you see
V is for vickle that's bickle° to me
W, watermelon that's coolin' mi dear
X is for extra that's finish here
Y is for yampi° and also yam°
Z is for zuzu° that a bwai° can nyam°

From: *Children's Jamaican Songs and Games* sung by Louise Bennett (Folkways Records).

Vocabulary
saltfish: fish preserved by drying and salting. Ackee and saltfish are often eaten together.
bammy: starchy cake made from grated cassava
dumpling: flour and water mixed to a dough, then boiled or baked
dokunu: cornmeal cake wrapped in a banana leaf
fufu: starchy paste made from pounded cooked cassava
injun cane: leafy green vegetable
jackfruit: large fruit with a strong smell
kingfruit: hybrid citrus fruit
lottus: tree bearing long brown pods, which contain seeds and a powdery yellow pulp. Also called "stinking toe" because of its smell.
ochro: okra
plantain: vegetable resembling a large banana, which is cooked before eating
Quashie: a country person. From the Twi name for a male child born on a Sunday.
rice and peas: rice and beans cooked together with coconut milk and spices. A favorite dish, also called the Jamaican Coat of Arms.
susumba: small round vegetable with a bitter taste
peg: segment
ugly: cross between a grapefruit and a tangerine. The name refers to the bumpy skin.
bickle: food
yampi, yam: starchy root vegetables
zuzu: meaning obscure
bwai: boy
nyam: eat

READING
Song of the Banana Man

BY EVAN JONES

Touris, white man, wipin' his face,
Met me in Golden Grove[0] market place.
He looked at m'ol' clothes brown wid stain[0],
An soaked right through wid de Portlan[0] rain,
He cas his eye, turn up his nose,
He says, "You're a beggar man, I suppose?"
He says, "Boy, get some occupation,
Be of some value to your nation."
    I said, "By God and dis big right han
    You mus recognize a banana man.

"Up in de hills, where de streams are cool,
An mullet[0] an janga[0] swim in de pool,
I have ten acres of mountain side[0],
An a dainty-foot donkey dat I ride,
Four Gros Michel[0], an four Lacatan[0],
Some coconut trees, an some hills of yam,
An I pasture on dat very same lan
Five she-goats and a big black ram.
    Dat, by God and dis big right han
    Is de property of a banana man.

"I leave m'yard[0] early-mornin time
An set m'foot to de mountain climb,
I ben m'back to de hot-sun toil
An m'cutlass rings on de stony soil,
Ploughin an weedin, diggin an plantin
Till Massa Sun[0] drop back o John Crow mountain,
Den home again in cool evenin time,
Perhaps whistling dis likkle rhyme,
    Praise God and m'big right han
    I will live an die a banana man.

"Banana day is my special day,
I cut my stems an I'm on m'way,
Load up de donkey, leave de lan
Head down de hill to banana stan,
When de truck comes roun I take a ride
All de way down to de harbor side—
Dat is de night, when you, touris man,
Would change your place wid a banana man.
    Yes, by God, an m'big right han

I will live an die a banana man.

"De bay is calm, an de moon is bright
De hills look black for de sky is light,
Down at de dock is an English ship[0],
Restin after her ocean trip,
While on de pier is a monstrous hustle,
Tallymen[0], carriers, all in a bustle,
Wid stems on deir heads[0] in a long black snake
Some singin de songs dat banana men make,
    Like, Praise God an m'big right han
    I will live an die a banana man.

"Den de payment comes, an we have some fun,
Me, Zekiel, Breda and Duppy Son.
Down at de bar near United Wharf
We knock back a white rum, bus a laugh
Fill de empty bag for further toil
Wid saltfish[0], breadfruit[0], coconut oil[0].
Den head back home to m'yard to sleep,
A proper sleep dat is long an deep.
    Yes, by God, an m'big right han
    I will live an die a banana man.

"So when you see dese ol clothes brown wid stain,
An soaked right through wid de Portland rain,
Don't cas your eye nor turn your nose,
Don't judge a man by his patchy clothes,
I'm a strong man, a proud man, an I'm free,
Free as dese mountains, free as dis sea,
I know myself, and I know my ways,
An will sing wid pride to de end o my days
    Praise God an m'big right han
    I will live an die a banana man."

–Reprinted from: Paula Burnett, ed., *The Penguin Book of Caribbean Verse in English* (Penguin Books Ltd., 1986).

Vocabulary

Golden Grove: town in eastern Jamaica
brown wid stain: banana trees produce a brown sap

Portland: parish on the north coast of Jamaica

mullet: type of fish

janga: crayfish

ten acres of mountain side: the banana farmers of Portland parish typically farmed steep hilly land

Gros Michel and Lacatan: varieties of banana

yard: home

Massa Sun: Master Sun

English ship: most Jamaican bananas are exported to England

tallymen: men who give checks or "tallies" to the banana growers to be redeemed for payment

stems on their heads: bananas used to be loaded on the ships by hand. Today they are mechanically packed and loaded.

saltfish: fish (usually cod) preserved by drying and salting

breadfruit: large starchy fruit

coconut oil: oil from the coconut, commonly used for cooking

Artist: Michelle Gibbs

UNIT SIX: From Rasta To Reggae
TEACHER GUIDE

▶ **OBJECTIVES**

Students will:

1. Explain how and why Rastafarianism emerged in Jamaica

2. Identify connections between Garveyism, Rastafarianism and reggae and relate these to the Pan-African tradition

▶ **QUESTIONS FOR DISCUSSION**

1. Have you ever seen or met a Rastafarian? What do they typically look like? What have you heard about them? On the basis of the reading, do you think what you heard is true?

2. How did this movement begin? What common themes can you identify between Rastafarianism and Marcus Garvey's movement?

3. Do any groups exist in your own community whose beliefs or lifestyle differ from the majority's? How are they viewed?

4. In which of the reggae songs can you find references to Rastafarian ideas? In which songs can you identify the influence of Pan-African ideas?

5. Contrast the song "African" by Peter Tosh to the poem "Back to Africa" by Louise Bennett [Unit 4]. Describe the attitudes toward the back-to-Africa movement reflected in each. How do they differ? What do you think is the reason for this?

6. Describe in your own words the main message of Oku Onuora's poem "Pressure Drop."

7. What is your favorite music? Why does it appeal to you? Can you identify any similarities to, or differences from, reggae?

▶ **SUGGESTED ACTIVITIES**

1. Invite members of Jamaican-American civic organization to visit the class and discuss the Rastafarian movement and other Jamaican cultural traditions. Such organizations are active in New York, Washington D.C., and other large cities. For help in locating one in your community, contact one of the national Jamaican organizations listed in the appendix.

Students should write their questions in advance. After the session, they will write how their ideas about Rastafarians have changed as a result of the readings and discussion.

2. It is important to the enjoyment of this unit that students have the opportunity to hear reggae music. Reggae albums and tapes are available in most record stores. Some classic LP's include: Desmond Dekker, *Israelites*; Max Romeo, *War in a Babylon*; Peter Tosh, *Witch Doctor*; Bunny Wailer, *Blackheart Man*; Judy Mowatt, *Black Woman*; Bob Marley and the Wailers, *Rastaman Vibra-*

tion, Natty Dread, Survival, and Uprising.

Play the songs in class as students follow along with the lyrics. After each song, ask students to explain its message in their own words and relate it to Jamaican social history. Students may also bring in other reggae records and play their favorite songs for the class.

▶ **RESOURCES**

1. Books on Rastafarians:

• Tracy Nicholas and Bill Sparrow, *Rastafari: A Way of Life* (Anchor Books, 1979). A sympathetic portrait of the Rastafarians through photographs and text.

• Joseph Owens, *Dread: The Rastafarians of Jamaica* (Sangster's Bookstores, 1976). The author lived among Rastafarians in Kingston and analyzes their theology and world-view. Senior high and above. Available from Heinemann.

• Roger Mais, *Brother Man* (Heinemann, 1974; first published 1954). Novel portraying life of the poor in Kingston and impact of early Rastafarians.

2. Stephen Davis and Peter Simon, *Reggae International* (Knopf, 1983). Beautifully illustrated book on reggae and its roots in Jamaican cultural history.

3. Collections of dub poetry include: Michael Smith, *Black and White*; Linton Kwesi Johnson, *Dread Beat and Blood*; Oku Onuora, *Echo*. Much dub poetry may be inaccessible to North American students because of its use of patois. Its typically raw language and blunt realism make it suitable for older students.

INTRODUCTION
From Rasta To Reggae

In the early 20th century, both the Ethiopianist religious movement and Marcus Garvey's Universal Negro Improvement Association urged Jamaicans to look to Africa [see Unit 3]. They called for an Africa free of colonial rule, which would be the rightful home of all people of African descent.

Ethiopia, as the only independent African country, was the focus of these longings. In 1930, a nobleman named Ras Tafari was crowned Emperor of Ethiopia. He took the name Haile Selassie. Soon, a number of Jamaicans, many of them poor rural dwellers, began calling Selassie the returned Messiah. They became known as Rastafarians.

After the Jamaican police broke up a rural Rastafarian settlement in 1954, many of its members moved to the ghetto areas of Kingston. There the movement took root, attracting members from the poorest strata of society.

The great majority of Jamaicans, some 70 percent, are Christians, members of churches such as the Roman Catholic, Anglican (Episcopal), Methodist and Baptist. Revivalism, a blend of African and European religious practices, also has many adherents. But Rastafarianism, although a minority cult, has broadened its appeal, attracting some students and professionals in addition to its base among the poor. "Rastas" can be found in every country of the English-speaking Caribbean and in the United States, Canada and England.

The Rastafarian Way of Life

Two beliefs are basic to Rastafarianism. One is that Haile Selassie is the living God (called "Jah"). The other is that Africa is the rightful home of all Blacks, and that liberation will

The lion, a Rastafarian symbol, represents Haile Selassie.

come through a return one day.

Rastafarians refer to the biblical story of the ancient Hebrews, who were enslaved, conquered and sent into exile in Babylon. They assert that this is actually their own story. For them, the ancient Hebrews were really Africans, who were enslaved and scattered to the four corners of the earth.

Rastafarians call Jamaica "Babylon" to emphasize that it is a land where they are held captive against their will. "Babylon" also refers to the institutions of Western society, especially the police. They refer to Ethiopia as "Zion," the promised land.

Rastafarian groups in the 1960s and 1970s attempted to arrange the repatriation of small groups of Jamaican Rastas to Africa, with varying degrees of success. Today most Rastafarians no longer emphasize a physical return to Africa. Instead, they focus on the need for changes within Jamaica, and on the liberation of Black people everywhere, especially in southern Africa.

In many ways, Rastafarians live like other working-class Jamaicans. Many are fishermen, farmers or artisans. But there are important differences. Rastafarians emphasize the beauty of African culture, and they have adopted various practices which they believe conform to a more natural and African way of living.

Many Rastas wear beards and long hair, called dreadlocks. They quote biblical passages prohibiting the cutting of hair. The official symbol of Haile Selassie is a lion, and Rastas sometimes compare their long locks to a lion's mane. Not all Rastafarians wear locks, however, and not everyone who wears them is a Rasta.

Rastafarians prefer to eat natural foods, especially vegetables and fruits. They consider meat harmful, and do not eat pork. They use many natural herbs for medicinal purposes.

Rastafarian society is male-dominated. Women generally are expected to remain at home caring for children, and to obey men. But this is gradually changing, as more Rasta women are demanding a dialogue with men about male and female roles within the movement.

Rastafarians criticize Jamaican society as colonial, oppressive and false. This rejection of the society's values has led some other Jamaicans, especially the middle and upper classes, to view the Rastafarians with hostility. During the 1950s and sixties, the Jamaican government harassed the Rastafarians. The Rastas' dreadlocks set them apart and made them an easy target for police brutality.

A more tolerant attitude developed during the 1970s. While not subscribing to Rastafarian beliefs, more Jamaicans came to recognize the Rasta message as a legitimate social critique. Rastas have also won admiration for their crafts and art. While still not fully accepting the Rastafarians, Jamaican society now recognizes their creative cultural contribution.

The Impact of Reggae

Another cultural trend of the 1970s helped spread the Rastafarian message. Reggae music was born in the poor neighborhoods of Kingston, and many songs tell of suffering in an unjust world. But reggae rose from these humble roots to become an international commercial success. In doing so, it brought Jamaican culture, including Rastafarianism, to the attention of the outside world.

A visitor describes a walk through West Kingston:

... The main street is dusty with no trees or greenery to break the piles of broken glass and rubbish. There are only long stretches of shacks. One corrugated iron fence was decorated with paintings of African leaders, including Obote, Banda, Kaunda, and, most importantly, Haile Selassie, the Conquering Lion of Judah who is the black God, Ras Tafari. One home stood out strikingly from the others, appearing to be constructed of ceramic tile in bright yellow and red. A closer look revealed it was created of hammered-out cheese tins.

... Everywhere, people were warm and friendly, shaking hands, chatting, drinking beer, or playing dominoes. One of the shacks had a small bar and jukebox inside. There, in the midst of pigs grunting at one's feet in the mud and slime, in the dirt and dust, people had their own jukeboxes, tape recorders and radios, all blaring out reggae, the voice of the ghetto.

–From Laura Tanna, Jamaican Folk Tales and Oral Histories (Institute of Jamaica, 1984).

Many influences contributed to the development of reggae. In the 1950s, Jamaicans listened to a soft music called *mento.* Many were also tuning their radios to U.S. stations to pick up popular songs, especially rhythm and blues. The influence of rhythm and blues on mento produced a new sound, *ska.*

During the 1960s, ska slowed and deepened to become *rock-steady.* As rock-steady absorbed other musical influences, especially soul, it gave way to a new music: reggae.

The migration from the rural areas to Kingston led to the growth of urban ghettoes and produced the so-called "rude-boys," unemployed youth who often led lives of petty crime. Early reggae tended to glorify the rude-boys as heroes, as in this song by the Slickers:

*Walking down the road,
with a pistol in your waist*

Johnny you're too bad

*Walking down the road,
with a ratchet in your waist*

Johnny you're too bad

*You're just a-robbing and stabbing
and looting and shooting*

Y'know you're too bad.

The rude-boy influence laid the basis for reggae's strident protest against poverty and racism. But the music goes beyond these negative themes to issue a positive call for the poor to "get up, stand up" and fight for their rights.

In the early 1970s, Bob Marley and the Wailers burst onto the reggae scene. Although the group split in 1973, its founding members—Bob Marley, Peter Tosh and Bunny Wailer—

Reggae artist Bob Marley

continued to dominate the reggae world. Bob Marley, who became an international superstar, used his music to send a strong message to Caribbean youth. In "Wake Up and Live," he echoes Marcus Garvey's call for united struggle by people of African descent:

Rise ye mighty people

There is work to be done

So let's do it little by little

Rise from your sleepless slumber

Another major influence on reggae was the Rastafarian movement. Rastafarian music, based on drumming, contributed reggae's trademark sound: a slow, powerful baseline with accents on the second and fourth beats. Reggae is permeated with Rastafarian symbols and themes. References to Jah, Babylon, Zion and repatriation to Africa are all woven into the music.

After Italy invaded Ethiopia in 1935, Haile Selassie made an eloquent appeal for help before the League of Nations. Decades later, Bob Marley used words from Selassie's speech as the lyrics for his song "War." The song, with its militant demand for an end to racism, brought reggae and Rastafarianism to the attention of the larger Black world.

Reggae spread from the Caribbean to England, where many Jamaicans had settled, then to the United States, Canada, and the Third World. Bob Marley performed at the independence celebrations for the African nation of Zimbabwe in 1980.

Since Marley's death from cancer in 1981, and the death of Peter Tosh in 1987, reggae has lost some of its hard-hitting message. But it has also helped lay the basis for new forms of cultural expression.

The most important is dub poetry. The dub poets, like Mutabaruka, Oku Onuora, Linton Kwesi Johnson and the late Michael Smith, focus on the experience of the urban poor. They speak their poems to a live audience, or "dub" them over a musical soundtrack. Both the serious social message and the rhythm of the spoken words relate dub poetry closely to reggae.

A related music trend, popular in Jamaican dance halls, is called "d.j. music." A disc jockey sings improvised lyrics into a microphone while the instrumental version (called the "dub version") of a popular song plays over the sound system. A d.j. who can come up with witty, rhyming lyrics is much admired. But some Jamaicans, especially those who grew up with reggae, criticize d.j. music as "slack," or empty of meaning.

Vocabulary

Obote: Milton Obote, first president of independent Uganda

Banda: Hastings Banda, first president of independent Malawi

Kaunda: Kenneth Kaunda, first president of independent Zambia

READING
Reggae Songs

"ONE DROP"
Bob Marley, from *Survival*

Feel it in the one drop
Well, I still find time to rap
We're making the one stop
The generation gap
So feel this drumbeat
As it beats within
Playing a rhythm
Resisting against the system

I know Jah[0] would never let us down
Pull your rights from wrong
I know Jah would never let us down
Oh no! Oh no!

They made their world so hard
Every day we got to keep on fighting
They made their world so hard
Every day the people are dying
It dread[0], dread for hunger and
Starvation dread dread, dread on dread
Lamentation dread dread
But read it in Revelation[0] dread dread
You'll find your redemption

Vocabulary

Jah: Rastafarian term for God

dread: Rastafarian term referring to the suffering of Blacks in colonial, white-dominated society. It has passed into common Jamaican speech to mean "terrible" or "oppressive." Rastafarians themselves are sometimes called "dreads."

Revelation: one of the books of the Bible. Rastafarians often cite its passages to support their beliefs.

"THE HARDER THEY COME"
Jimmy Cliff, from *The Harder They Come*

O they tell me of a pie up in the sky

Waiting for me when I die
But between the day you're born and when you die
They never seem to hear you when you cry
    So as sure as the sun will shine
    I'm gonna get my share now, what's mine
    And then the harder they come, the harder they fall
One and all
    Ooh the harder they come, the harder they fall
One and all

Well the oppressors are trying to keep me down
Trying to drive me underground
And they think that they have got the battle won
I say forgive them, Lord, they know not what they've done
    Because as sure as the sun will shine (etc.)

And I keep on fighting for the things I want
Though I know that when you're dead you can't
But I'd rather be a free man in my grave
Than living as a puppet or a slave
    So as sure as the sun will shine (etc.)

"ZION TRAIN"
Bob Marley, from *Uprising*

Zion[0] train is coming our way

Oh people get on board
You better get on board
Thank the Lord, Praise Fari[0]
I gotta catch this train
'Cause there is no other station
Then you going in the same direction.

Zion train is coming our way.
Which man can save his brother soul
Oh man, it's just self control
Don't gain the world and lose your soul
Wisdom is better than silver and gold
To the rich.

Where there is a will, there is always a way
Where there is a will, there's always a way.
Zion train is coming our way.

Two thousand years of history

Could not be wiped away so easily
Two thousand years of history, Black history
Could not be wiped away so easily.

Oh children, Zion train is coming our way
Get on board now, Zion train is coming our way
You got a ticket so thank the Lord.

Vocabulary

Zion: Rastafarian term for Ethiopia, equated with the biblical promised land

Fari: Ras Tafari, original name of Haile Selassie

"REDEMPTION SONG"
Bob Marley, from *Uprising*

Old pirate yes they rob I
Sold I to the merchant ships
Minutes after they took I
From the bottomless pit
But my hand was made strong
By the hand of the Almighty
We forward in this generation triumphantly

Won't you help to sing these songs of freedom
'Cause all I ever had
Redemption songs, redemption songs.

Emancipate yourselves from mental slavery
None but ourselves can free our mind
Have no fear for atomic energy
'Cause none a them can stop the time

How long shall they kill our prophets
While we stand aside and look
Some say it's just a part of it
We've got to fulfill the book.

Won't you help to sing these songs of freedom
'Cause all I ever had, redemption songs
All I ever had, redemption songs
These songs of freedom, songs of freedom.

"WAR"
Bob Marley, from *Rastaman Vibration*

Until the philosophy which holds
One race superior and another inferior
Is finally and permanently discredited
And abandoned
There is war, everywhere is war

That until there are no longer
First class and second class
Citizens of any nation
Until the color of a man's skin
Is of no more significance
Than the color of his eyes
Is a war

That until their basic human rights
Are equally guaranteed to all
Without regard to race
There's a war

That until that day
The dream of lasting peace, world citizenship

From the jacket of Bob Marley's album Uprising

And the rule of international morality
Will remain but a fleeting illusion
To be pursued but never attained
Now everywhere is war

And until the ignoble and unhappy
Regimes that now hold our brothers
In Angola, in Mozambique⁰, South Africa
In subhuman bondage
Have been toppled, utterly destroyed
Everywhere is war

Until that day the African continent
Will not know peace
We Africans will fight, we find it necessary
And we know we shall win
As we are confident in the victory
Of good over evil, good over evil.

Vocabulary

Angola, Mozambique: African countries
under Portuguese colonial rule at the time of
Selassie's speech

"AFRICAN"
Peter Tosh, from *Equal Rights*

Don't care where you come from
As long as you're a Black man, you're an African
No mind your nationality

Reggae artist Peter Tosh

You have got the identity of an African

Cause if you come from Clarendon⁰, you are an African
And if you come from Portland⁰, you are an African
And if you come from Westmoreland⁰, you are an African

Cause if you come from Trinidad, you are an African
And if you come from Nassau⁰, you are an African
And if you come from Cuba, you are an African

No mind your complexion
There is no rejection, you are an African
Cause if your 'plexion high, high, high,
If you 'plexion low, low, low,
And if your 'plexion in between
You are African
No mind denomination
That is only segregation, you are an African
Cause if you go to the Catholic, you are an African
Or if you go to the Methodist, you are an African
And if you go to the Church of God, you are an African

Cause if you come from Brixton⁰, you are an African
And if you come from Neasden⁰, you are an African
And if etc. (with Willesden⁰, Bronx, Brooklyn,
Queens, Manhattan, Canada, Miami, Switzerland,
Germany, Russia, Taiwan ...)

Vocabulary

Clarendon, Portland, Westmoreland:
parishes (counties) of Jamaica

Nassau: capital of the Bahamas

Brixton, Neasden, Willesden: districts of
London where many Caribbean emigrants
have settled

"AFRICA UNITE"
Bob Marley, from *Survival*

Africa unite
'Cause we're moving right out of Babylon⁰
And we're going to our fathers' land

How good and how pleasant it would be
Before God and man to see
The unification of all Africans
As it's been said already
Let it be done right now

We are the children of the Rastaman
We are the children of the higher man

So Africa unite, Africa unite yeah
Africa unite
'Cause we're moving right out of Babylon
And we're grooving to our fathers' land

How good and how pleasant it would be
Before God and man to see
The unification of all Rastaman
As it is been said let it be done
I tell you who we are under the sun
We are the children of the Rastaman
We are the children of the higher man

So Africa unite, Africa unite yeah
Africa unite 'cause the children want
To come home, Africa unite, Africa unite
It's later, later than you think
It's later, later than you think
Unite for the benefit of your people
Unite for the Africans abroad
Unite for the Africans a yard[0]

Vocabulary

Babylon: Rastafarian term for western society

Africans a yard: Africans here in Jamaica

"DEM BELLY FULL"
Written by Legon Cogil and Carlton Barrett, performed by Bob Marley on *Natty Dread*

Dem belly full but we 'ungry
A hungry mob is a hangry mob
De rain a fall but de dutty[0] tough
A pot a cook but de food nuh 'nough
   We're gonna dance to Jah music, yeh
   We're gonna dance to Jah music, yeh
   Forget your sorrows and dance
   Forget your troubles and dance
   Forget your sickness and dance
   Forget your weariness and dance
Ah say: cost of living get so high
De rich and poor dey start to cry
And now de weak must get strong by singing
Ah what a tribulation
Sing: muh belly full but me hungry
A hungry man is a hangry man
A rain a fall but de dutty tough

A pot a cook but de food nuh 'nough
   We're gonna chuck to Jah music, we're chuckin, yeh
   You hear we're chuckin to Jah music, we're chuckin

Vocabulary

dutty: dirt, ground

READING

Pressure Drop

A DUB POEM BY OKU ONUORA

hunga a twis man tripe[0]
just say 'eh'
man fight
man nerves raw
man tek a draw   cool
man jook up a tek in de scene
garbage dead-daag[0] fly
"cho[0]! but dis nuh right"
man ready fe explode
man cyaan[0] bear de load
                    pressure drop

dahta sigh
"lard! hear de pickney[0] dem a cry"
man a pass say dahta fat
dahta smile
but dahta cyaan check dat[0]
dahta haffi[0] a check fe food fe put ina pat[0]
dahta say all man want a fe get im han[0] under skirt
bam! say she a breed[0]
im vanish like when you bun[0] weed
dahta wan wuk[0]
dahta willin fe wuk
but is like say dahta nuh have nuh luck
or dem nuh have enough wuk?
dahta say she nah ketch nu men
she say she nah falla nu fren[0]
dahta confuse
too often dahta get use
dahta bahl[0]
"lard! weh me a go do?"
                    pressure drop

man flare
ina de slum man haffi live mongs rat, roach, fly, chink[0]
"cho! de place stink"
man willin fe wuk
man nuh wan fe bun gun ina man gut
man nuh jus wan fe jook up an chat
man nuh wan fe pap lack[0]
but when hunger twis tripe an pickney bahl
time dread
eart tun red

curfew
man screw
gun blaze
knife flash
man run hot
        when pressure drop

—Reprinted from: Orlando Wong [Oku Onuora], *Echo* (Sangster's Book Stores, 1977).

Vocabulary

tripe: stomach, guts

daag: dog

cho!: exclamation of anger or impatience

cyaan: can't

dahta: woman (from "daughter")

pickney: child, children

cyaan check dat: can't pay attention to that

haffi: has to

pat: pot

im han: his hand

breed: become pregnant

bun: burn

wuk: work

she nah falla nu fren: she won't follow a new friend, i.e., take on a new boyfriend

bahl: cry (bawl)

chink: hole in the roof

pap lack: steal ("pop lock")

UNIT SEVEN: Women's Theater in Jamaica
TEACHER GUIDE

▶ **OBJECTIVES**

Students will:

1. Appreciate the Jamaican arts tradition through drama

2. Identify several major problems facing women and solutions they have found

3. Analyze the importance of community-based organizations in movements for social change

▶ **QUESTIONS FOR DISCUSSION**

1. How has Jamaican theater changed since colonial times? What do you think were the reasons for these changes?

2. How and why did the Sistren Theater Collective begin? What do members of the group have in common?

3. How do they make their plays? What are the plays about?

4. Have you ever had a problem that you thought was yours alone, and then discovered that others had similar difficulties? How did that affect you? When other women recognize themselves in the Sistren plays, how can this help bring about change?

5. Why did Gloria adopt two children when she could not afford to feed them? Why did the children's mother bring them to Gloria? What does this tell you about Gloria?

6. Why can't Gloria get a job that pays well? What kind of work did she try before the children got sick? What went wrong?

7. Why does the landlady end up admiring Gloria and Ruth?

8. What message does the play convey to you? Is any aspect of this message relevant to your own life?

▶ **SUGGESTED ACTIVITIES**

1. A group of students performs the skit "Tribute to Gloria Who Overcame Death." It is not necessary to use the original dialogue; students may substitute their own words.

2. The class writes and performs a skit exposing a common problem in their school or community and proposing a solution. The following steps are suggested:

   a) The class brainstorms to identify a problem in the school or community, or a larger social problem, which will be the subject of the skit. Remind students that their goal is not to criticize individuals, but to make people aware of a common problem and propose ways to work together to solve it.

b) Collectively develop a basic story line. Outline it on the chalkboard.

c) Each member of the class develops a character that he/she wants to portray. Refine the story further.

d) Act out the skit on an improvised basis. Have one or two members of the class take notes.

e) A team of two writers is chosen to script the skit, based on the improvisation. The class reviews the draft, then revises to incorporate suggestions.

f) Using the final script, perform the skit. It may be videotaped.

▶ RESOURCES

1. Sistren Theater Collective with Honor Ford-Smith, ed., *Lionheart Gal: Life Stories of Jamaican Women* (The Women's Press, 1986). Autobiographical narratives by members of Sistren. The use of patois makes this suitable for advanced students.

INTRODUCTION
Women's Theater in Jamaica

"Caribbean theater has become today a source of pride. It is one area of our lives in which we are genuinely beginning to applaud each other. Standing ovations are no longer reserved for the players from outside."

So wrote Trevor Rhone, a Jamaican playwright who is one of the Caribbean's leading dramatists. His popular play *Smile Orange* was later made into a movie. Rhone's words reflect his pride in Jamaica's vibrant cultural movement, of which theater is an important part.

The first public theater was built in Jamaica in 1682. Like other Caribbean theaters during the colonial era, it staged English plays for an audience made up mainly of colonial settlers from England.

Beginning in the 1930s, Jamaican theater became more oriented to the Caribbean experience. A 1937 production, *Jamaica Triumphant*, dramatized the island's history. Marcus Garvey's Universal Negro Improvement Association sponsored an open-air stage in Kingston, where Black actors starred in plays about Jamaican life.

In the 1940s the Little Theater Movement began staging the annual Jamaica Pantomime. This was not actually a pantomime, but a colorful performance of music, dance and drama. When the Pantomime opened in 1943 with *Jack and the Beanstalk*, virtually the only Black face among the performers was

Sistren performing "Trickster and de Muffet Posse," a play about women's struggles against violence.

that of the actress who played the witch.

Eventually the Pantomime became Jamaicanized, however, and today Black actors predominate. Still performed every year at Christmas, the Pantomime draws its themes from the Jamaican folk tradition, particularly the Anansi tales.

Today, one can always find high-quality drama by Jamaican and foreign playwrights playing in Kingston theaters. Some Jamaican dramatists train at the Cultural Training Centre's School of Drama, or at the University of the West Indies. Others, like the women in the Sistren Theater Collective, draw on their own life experiences as the basis for creating authentic Caribbean drama.

The Sistren Theater Collective

SISTREN, which means "sisters," is a women's cultural organization in Kingston, Jamaica. It includes the only theater company in the Caribbean that has developed from the initiative of working-class women. Through drama, Sistren educates the public about problems facing women and helps bring pressure for change.

Unlike traditional theater companies, which most often work from published scripts, Sistren's members create their own plays. They deal with topics like violence against women, teenage pregnancy, and the unfair treatment of women in the workplace. The group performs throughout the Caribbean, and has toured the United States, Europe and Canada.

Sistren also holds workshops with community groups, helping them use drama to understand and confront the particular problems they face. There is a textile project which produces original silk-screened designs. The group has published a collection of the life stories of its members, entitled *Lionheart Gal.*

Sistren's success was built on humble roots. The original 13 members came together in 1977 while being trained as teachers' aides in a Jamaican government program to provide jobs for unemployed workers. All had experienced poverty. Many of the women had been abused or abandoned by male partners, and were on their own with children to support. Lillian Foster's experience was typical.

I am from Kingston. I went to Kingston Technical High School, and I went the domestic science way—nowadays they call it home economics—so that I could get into Kingston Public Hospital to train as a nurse. But I started having children from an early stage, and that is what blighted my prospects.

When I had the first child, the trouble started. [My godmother] didn't want to keep me, but you know, she looked it over and I stayed there. But when I find myself pregnant with the second one, I was thrown out.

At that time, the father of my first and second child was getting ready to go to England. And this other man, seeing that I was pregnant, decided to take

me with this pregnancy. He rented a room and put both of us in there ... I got my clothes, my food, everything that I needed.

But he was sort of on the rough side. He was very jealous. He didn't want me to talk to anyone, neither a man nor a woman. And it go on and on, and I found myself pregnant with my third child. But finally I couldn't take his jealousy, and I had to leave him when my son was six months old.

So there I was at home, not working. And this Special Employment Program came up. I said, "Well, let me go and do it, because I'll be working for my honest bread." Soon after that, Sistren started, in 1977. And I'm in it until now.

The thirteen women were asked to put on a play for the annual Workers' Week celebrations. They approached the Jamaican School of Drama for a director to help prepare their performance, and met Honor Ford-Smith. When she asked, "What do you want to do a play about?" they answered, "We want to do plays about how we suffer as women."

Talking about their lives that day led to "Downpression Get A Blow," a play about women workers in a garment factory who form a union and win their demands. From that performance, Sistren was born.

Their first major production was "Bellywoman Bangarang[0]." It presented the life stories of four pregnant women, raising questions of rape, domestic violence, and domestic work. It showed how unemployment and poverty were at the root of these problems. Lillian Foster remembers:

We do our plays by improvisation. We take our own experience—teenage pregnancy, mother and child experiences and so on—and we put bits and pieces together to form the play. And we make up our own songs. Yes man, it's fantastic! Then we write a script, but what is written in the script comes from what we say.

Our first major production was about teenage pregnancy. We saw teenagers going to school, getting pregnant, mother turning them out; and the man getting them pregnant and leaving them alone to bring up this child. It's a real mixed-up thing. So we call the play "Bellywoman Bangarang," because we always like to give our plays a funny name.

Sistren's plays show not only the problems women face, but also their resourcefulness in solving them. One such play is "Tribute to Gloria Who Overcame Death." A young Jamaican mother is left without support when her man migrates to the United States. Her four children—two of her own, and two she has adopted—become sick and weak from hunger. Death appears in the person of an old woman, and tells Gloria she will return in a month to take the children away.

Frightened, Gloria takes her children across the island and moves in with her sister Ruth. Together, the two women devise a plan to fool Death.

Like many Jamaican women with children to care for, Gloria and Ruth cannot get jobs that pay good salaries. They must use their ingenuity to make ends meet. Gloria goes to the market and begins to make a little money as a higgler. Each day she buys a large bunch of bananas and divides it into smaller bunches, selling each for a few pennies more than it cost her.

Gloria and Ruth also make candies and sell them, and Ruth works part-time as a maid in a wealthy home. They plant a garden of vegetables and fruits, and feed the children these nutritious foods. When Death returns, she finds the children fat and healthy, and concludes she has the wrong house. Through their determination and hard work, Gloria and Ruth have overcome Death.

Vocabulary

bellywoman: pregnant woman

bangarang: confusion, quarrel or riot

READING
Tribute To Gloria Who Overcame Death

A ONE-ACT PLAY BY THE SISTREN THEATER COLLECTIVE

Narrator: Time was, in the heart of the ghetto ...

Actress One: In the district of Hope Hill ...

Actress Two: In a one Whappen Bappen° house ...

Actress Three: Beside the gully ...

Actress Four: In the housing scheme° government just done build ...

Narrator:
>There was a woman
>Just an ordinary sister
>Black skin, full lips, hair cut low
>Cane rowed or afroed
>An ordinary sister
>Named Gloria.

>(*Enter Gloria*)

>Gloria (singing):
>My touch is rough as the bark of a tree
>Fingers twisted with work like the ginger root.
>Take my arm and feel the strength
>Of the women who have sown the seed of
>life in you.
>Take my hand and feel the courage
>Of the women who have loved the dream of
>life in you.

SCENE ONE

Narrator: Gloria had a daughter.

Gloria: Angela! But what a pickney° to read book sir!

Narrator: And a son.

Gloria: Victor! But why that little boy won't stay in the yard though! From morning the shoes don't clean yet.

Artist: Juan C. Urquiola

Narrator: And she had two more children she had taken to care for. For instance, take Pepita.

(*Enter neighbor with child*)

Neighbor: Pepita! Shut up you mouth or me going lick you again.

Gloria: Morning, Maudlyn.

Neighbor: Oh, Miss Gloria. Me never see you. Is you me come to.

Gloria: Eeehee?⁰ Me no have no extra flour this morning.

Neighbor: Is not that me come about, ma'am. Them send telegram for me, ma'am.

Gloria: Poor thing. Who dead now? Don't is just last week you borrow two dollar from me to go to you uncle funeral in town?

Neighbor: Is the hotel people me used to work for. Them send for me to start work for them again. Them want me to come tonight!

Gloria: Eeehee? What a pity you no have nobody to leave Pepita with.

Neighbor: Is that me did really come to you about, ma'am.

Gloria: Me no know nobody, not a soul! And furthermore, me no like gal pickney⁰.

Neighbor: She like you, ma'am. Look how she smile pon you. From she little she did always a-stick on to you.

Gloria: Eeehee? Dark sugar gone up again this week.

Neighbor: If me no take the work tonight, ma'am, them going give it to somebody else.

Gloria: Tin milk⁰ gone up too.

Neighbor: Me a-beg you, Miss G ... Me will come back soon as me find somewhere else to put her.

Gloria: The Lord said suffer the little children to come unto me.

Narrator: And Gloria had the baby who also wasn't hers.

Gloria: Angie. The baby's mother come back?

Angie: No, mama.

Gloria: She send a message?

Angie: No, mama.

Gloria: You better go back look for her again.

Angie: Might as well we keep him. You no see she nah come again?

Gloria: (*to the baby*) Me no like boy pickney. See there! Him wet me up again. Me a-go carry you down a police station right now. What them going do with you? You mighta grow up to beat up poor people. Better me carry you down a children's home. But nobody nah take you. After milk gone up again ... You mother wicked like ... and she miserable. If you ever grow up and take after ... Lawd! Him smiling. Angie come quick, the baby smiling for the first time!

SCENE TWO

Narrator: One day her man up and went off to America on the farm work scheme⁰. Gloria, her neighbor and her friend went to see him off on his journey.

Neighbor: Ah, how so much man a-go way ...

Gloria: See him there!

Friend: Him a-wave.

Gloria: Him fix himself good eh? Me heart feel full. Alright! Safe travel. Member when you write to send the letter go to Miss P ... Yes!

Friend: Watch Miss James' son, me never know him a-go way too.

Gloria: Him still a-wave. John! John! No bother make them find any fault with you and send you back. Him gone in. Him gone in.

Neighbor: After all, him can't stay outside and just a-look pon you so.

Gloria: No, me did want him stay little longer. Feel me heart, feel how it a-beat. Me a-go miss him. No matter the money. Me only want to know-say him come back. When the pickney come to me and say Mama, Papa nah come back? What me a-go say? Me sorry me encourage him to go.

Neighbor: If him back with money, it alright. If him no have none, him can stay there. Come, no fret yourself. Come we go take a shot a whites⁰ to get the feelings outa you.

SCENE THREE

Narrator: Gloria was very miserable. She couldn't find any food to give the children.

Gloria: Angela, me no tell you to put down the school book, you nah go a school today for me no have no lunch money. Victor— you better come inside and clean you shoes and pick up you clothes or I going send you out naked tomorrow. Stop pinching the baby, Pepita. Angela, watch them while me gone. Me a-look work.

Narrator: She tried all kinds of work. She tried domestic work⁰.

Madam: Late again, and what's more you've been taking home my condensed milk! Do you think I pay you thirty dollars a week to have you eat me out of house and home? I said no meals. You're fired, and don't expect a reference from me!

Narrator: She tried a building site.

Gloria: Please sir. Me a-look work. Me strong and ...

Foreman: Sorry baby, men only.

Narrator: Gloria couldn't feed her children and they got sick.

CHORUS
(Sneezes)
Mama mama me hungry
Mama mama me belly a hot me
Mama mama me want water, mama mama me hungry.

Narrator: She didn't know what to do.

(*Gloria cries*)

Narrator: One night Gloria dreamed of death.

Gloria: Who's there?

Death: An old woman, me knows you well.

Gloria: Who you?

Death: Long time me watching you now. Open the door. I thirsty. Is late at night and I coming from far far off.

Gloria: Me no entertain strangers this hour of the night.

Death: But after me know you family so well ... you mother Sarah. You Aunty Gem, and you Granny.

Gloria: But all a them dead!

Death: What a lovely set of children. Let me stretch out on the bed beside them. In the morning them can follow me which part me a-go⁰. An old woman like me needs plenty help.

(*Death lies on bed*)

Gloria: Angie what do you? What mek you a tremble so? Victor! me pickney! Who you? What you want?

Death: (*rises ... laughs*) Day soon light. Me a-carry them now. Make a-see. Victor, Angela, Pepita and the baby. Eeehee!

Gloria: But what is this? Where them can go in them sick sick state?

Death: A me them belongs to now.

Gloria: Where you a-carry them?

Death: When me come back for you, that time you will know.

Gloria: Who you?

Death: No look pon me face if you want to survive.

Narrator: Gloria understood that she was face to face with death.

Gloria: Wait. Sit down likkle⁰. Drink some water. Me really no like to see the pickney them a-suffer. If you take them it might be the best.

Death: Now you talking sense.

Gloria: But in so far as me see it, them no have no use to you the way them is now.

Death: Why?

Gloria: Last week me send Angie for likkle water and the way she weak she could hardly carry it up the hill.

Death: She no go need water which part she a-go.

Gloria: How them going work for you if them so weak?

Death: A true. Is the hardest thing to get people to work in these times. Me have one set a lazy people, me can't get them to do nothing.

Gloria: That's why you not to burden yourself with these. Them will only give you more trouble.

Death: Take care, you a-try to set me up!

Gloria: Look pon them yourself.

Death: Them mawga⁰ for true. An me just get a whole heap a boy who dead inna the political violence⁰. The whole a them mawga. Then me get some a the pickney with the polio and them foot hook up so them slow too.

Gloria: Let me ask you something. Leave them for one month. Me will fatten them up. Then you can take them.

Death: A fool you a-try to fool me or what?

Gloria: That time them can look after you.

Death: (takes out notebook) One month. Make a-see. That time me coming back for (to audience) you ... you ... and you.

Gloria: Me will dress them up, make them stay good. Ready for you.

Death: Me going come back. Next time the moon full. You better keep you promise or me will carry you with me when we meet again.

SCENE FOUR

Narrator: Gloria knew she had to move fast.

Gloria: Angie come darling, try pack up you books. Victor, wrap up warm. Pepita! Sit still while me put on you clothes. Angie, try hold the baby for me. Hurry up, come make haste. Angie, you put the pot in the bag yet? Victor, open you eye!

Narrator: Out into the darkness of the foreday morning they went. Gloria weighed down with coal pot and the few little pieces of clothes they had. Before the cock crow with only the peeney wallies⁰ to guide them, they walked away from the path of death.

Victor: Where we going Mama?

Gloria: To the other side of the island. Pepita! Take that stone out you mouth. (They get into a mini-bus⁰.) One stop, driver.

Conductor⁰: Wait-a-bit, Green Island, Lucea, Montego Bay. Come in nuh lady. Bust it, driver!

(Minibus drives)

Gloria: One stop driver!

Conductor: Come on mother, you a-take too long. Bust it, driver!

Narrator: All day they rode in minibus after minibus. All day they walked in the hot sun, the breeze flinging them here and there, dust blowing in the children's faces. All day they flagged down cars and buses.

Gloria: Me beg you a drive sir. The children sick and them can't walk no more.

Driver: But you must be mad to be walking pon street with sick children!

Narrator: Late in the afternoon they arrived at the home of Gloria's sister. But Ruth was in a sticky situation.

Landlady: How long you expect me to wait for the rent?

Neighbor: Me a-warn you. If you damn chicken come mess pon me front step one more time, you watch me and you.

Ruth: But, but me tell you …

Landlady: No bother tell me nothing. Is money me a-deal with.

Neighbor: If you can't control you pickney (Gloria knocks) them going have to put up with whatever me do them.

Ruth: Wait. Gloria, a really you!

Neighbor: A who she?

Landlady: Me only hope she no come to come pack up the yard with that whole heap a ticky-ticky⁰ pickney.

Neighbor: What a way them bad. This one favor sailorman pickney⁰. Mind what kind a people you have coming in you yard Miss Doneyfield, for me a one Christian woman … Ouch!

Gloria: Pepita. No step pon the woman toe.

Landlady: Me a-warn you for the last time, Ruth.

Artist: Vernal Reuben

Neighbor: Think them can go on with them slackness⁰ … (They exit.)

Ruth: Gloria me glad to see you, but chile, hard time a-beat me.

Narrator: The two sisters talked for hours. They made a plan. They decided to work together to overcome death.

Gloria: Put it there sister! (They shake.) We a-go win through.

Narrator: So the next day, Ruth took Gloria to the market where she worked.

First Market Vendor: Buy you Sunday morning breakfast!

Second Market Vendor: Dollar a pound for tomato. Me nah sell no half pound of carrot. Dollar fifty a pound for carrot. Me nah sell thyme without scallion.

Narrator: Gloria bought a stem of green bananas⁰. She cut it up and sold it in small bunches. Each time one stem finished, she bought another and sold it. Each time she made a small profit.

Gloria: Lady with the bag, buy you green banana. Gentleman in the red shoes, buy something nuh … Cho⁰! You favor poppy show⁰. Wait! Thief! Thief! (chases thief)

Narrator: When they came home in the evening, they brought food for the children.

Gloria: Victor! Come for your dinner.

Narrator: Ruth planted yam⁰ and callaloo⁰ outside the house.

Landlady: Me no want you to come dig up dig up me yard. Ouch!

Gloria: Pepita. You have to learn to stop bite people.

Narrator: In the evening they stayed up late making candy and potato pudding.

Ruth: Victor! Stop thiefing the grater coconut⁰.

Narrator: Gloria put the sweets on her head and sold them at the school gate.

Gloria: (*calling to customers*) Toto⁰, flah flah⁰, candy, grater cake⁰!

Narrator: And in the evening, they fed the children.

Gloria: Angie, eat one more dumplin⁰ darling.

Ruth: Victor, don't you dare leave that piece of breadfruit⁰ on the plate.

Gloria: Pepita, eat you rice and peas⁰.

Ruth: Now for dessert, some sweet potato pudding.

Neighbor: But a what this! You a-overfeed you pickney. The Lord said gluttonous is one of the seven deadly sins.

Gloria: And him also said thou shalt not fast in thy neighbor's business⁰!

Narrator: After a while ...

Ruth: Me get day's work⁰.

Gloria: How much them a-pay you?

Ruth: No much, but them have a big pantry and me going carry home condense milk and rice.

Gloria: Rope in star. Pepita! Eat every piece of that yam.

SCENE FIVE

Narrator: Angela, Victor, Pepita and the baby began to grow round and healthy. On the night of the full moon, the sisters were very busy.

Gloria: Angie, you have on Victor's clothes?

Angie: Yes, Mama.

Gloria: Then come out make I see you nuh pickney.

Ruth: She favor boy pickney⁰ for true! Put Sarah between Pepita and the baby.

Gloria: Victor, come out a the bathroom.

Victor: Me nah come out inna the gal-pickney clothes.

Ruth: Put Roy between Angie and Victor.

Gloria: And put Marcus and Pepita down the foot of the bed.

Ruth: Good, how them look?

Gloria: A who them? A no fi-me pickney⁰.

Narrator: The two women hid behind the dresser to watch for Death. When the moon was bright and high in the sky, in the early hours just before the sun came up, Death entered the house.

Death: (*laughs*)

Gloria: (*whispers*) Ruth, wake up, she come!

Ruth: (*mumbles in sleep*)

Gloria: (*claps hand over her mouth*)

Death: What a way the place dark! But what a heap a healthy looking pickney. Just what I need. Make me see now. Angela ... no .. must be this ... no ... dis one a boy. Wait likkle. Victor ... cho! ... where him there ... no ... this one a gal pickney ... and she too fat ... Angela did have ringworm in her head. But wait me no see the mother neither ...

Gloria: (*sneezes*)

Ruth: (*jumps up and claps hand over her mouth*)

Death: A who that? ... Hmmmmm ... A wonder if it could be the wrong house me have. Make me look and see if anything look familiar. Me remember Pepita did have a pair of red shoes.

Gloria: (*rushes out when back is turned and grabs shoes*)

Death: Must be the wrong house.

Gloria: (*sneezes again*)

Death: Wait. A what that! (She passes right in front of Gloria.) Well as long as me come me might as well take these. This likkle one look good. OUCH! What that! (Death falls.)

Gloria: Pepita trip her!

Ruth: Roy thump her!

Gloria: Angie bite her! Go deh me pickney!

Death: Wait! Wait! Do me I beg yuh! Stop! All right, all right. Me no want you any more. (Death rises, straightens clothes.) After all me have plenty work to do and me don't have no time to waste.

Narrator: And so Death passed them by.

Gloria: Put it deh, star!

Ruth: What you say!

(*much rejoicing and laughing*)

(*Neighbor and Landlady knock at the door.*)

Landlady: Miss G., me come to beg you look pon me pickney because one a them sick and me no know how to better him. Me see Angie did have one sore last week and me have to admire how you and Ruth did better it.

Neighbor: Them must did carry pickney a obeahman⁰. Mind how you chat to obeahwoman.

Landlady: Shut up you mouth. You too bad-minded. If anything, she a miracle worker. Tell me you secret Miss G., Miss Ruth, for me woulda really like to know how you manage look after you pickney so good even though you not working.

Gloria: Well ...

Narrator: And many others came to congratulate Gloria and Ruth on their lovely children ... There are many more women like Gloria all over Jamaica.

Actress One: In the ghetto ...

Actress Two: In the mountains and valleys ...

Actress Three: In Whappen Bappen houses ...

Actress Four: In gullies ...

Actress Five: In housing schemes ...

Narrator: (*sings*)
  Ordinary women
  Black skin, full lips,
  Hair cane rowed or afroed
  Ordinary miracle-working women ...
  Who look after us day after day.

–"Tribute to Gloria Who Overcome Death," a one-act play by the Sistren Theater Collective. Scriptwriter: Honor-Ford Smith. Original cast: Jasmin Smith, Myrtle Thompson, Lana Finikin, Beverley Hanson, Cerene Stephenson, Vivette Lewis. Script adapted for this collection.

Members of the Sistren Theater Collective

Vocabulary

Whappen Bappen house: shack made from scraps of wood, cardboard or metal

housing scheme: housing project for poor families

pickney: child, children

eehee?: oh really?

gal pickney: girl child

tin milk: canned condensed milk, a staple food of the poor

farm work scheme: program to recruit Jamaican men as temporary farm laborers in the United States, usually to cut sugar cane or pick fruit

shot a whites: drink of white rum

domestic work: work as a servant in someone's home

which part me a-go: where I'm going

likkle: little

mawga: thin

the political violence: The period before the 1980 election in Jamaica was marked by gang warfare between supporters of the opposing parties. Up to 800 people died.

peeney wallies: fireflies

minibus: small van, the main form of transport between towns in Jamaica

conductor: person who collects fares from minibus passengers

ticky ticky: thin

this one favor sailorman pickney: this one looks like a sailor's child (i.e. neglected)

slackness: irresponsible, undisciplined ways

green banana: unripe bananas to be cooked and eaten as a starch

Cho!: exclamation of anger or impatience

you favor poppy show: a mild insult

yam: starchy root vegetable

callaloo: leafy green vegetable, like spinach

grater coconut: grated coconut

toto: small cake

flah flah: codfish fritters

grater cake: cake made from grated coconut

dumplin: boiled dumpling made of flour and water

breadfruit: starchy fruit eaten boiled, roasted or fried

rice and peas: rice and beans, a common Jamaican dish

fast in thy neighbor's business: interfere in your neighbor's business

day's work: work as a domestic servant

she favor boy pickney: she looks like a little boy

fi-me pickney: my children

obeahman, obeahwoman: practitioner of witchcraft (the neighbor is suggesting that Gloria had the children cured by means of magic)

Sources of Classroom Materials

► **PUBLISHERS AND DISTRIBUTORS**

Africa World Press, Inc./The Red Sea Press, Inc., 11-D Princess Road, Lawrenceville, NJ 08648. (800) 789-1898 or (609) 844-9583, fax (609) 844-0198. awprsp@africanworld.com www.africanworld.com *Fiction and nonfiction.*

Caribbean Books, PO Box 680, Parkersburg, IA 50665. (888) 396-6354. *Distributes a wide variety of books on the Caribbean.*

Greenwood/Heinemann Publishing Group, 88 Post Road West, Westport, CT 06881. (800) 793-2154, fax (203) 222-1502. www.heinemann.com *Fiction and non-fiction.*

Addison Wesley Longman Ltd., 1 Jacob Way, Reading, MA 01867. (800) 824-7799. *Fiction and non-fiction. Publishes* Caribbean Story, *a two-volume illustrated history of the Caribbean for secondary schools.*

Monthly Review Press, 122 West 27ᵗʰ Street, New York, NY 10001. (800) 670-9499 or (212) 691-2555. mreview@igc.apc.org *Nonfiction.*

NYU Press, 70 Washington Square South, New York, New York 10012. (800) 996-6987, fax (212) 995-3833. www.nyupress.nyu.edu *Distributor for Monthly Review Press titles as well as books published by the Latin American Bureau in London, including short profiles of several Caribbean countries.*

South End Press, 7 Brookline Street, #1, Cambridge, MA 02139-4146. (800) 533-8478, fax (617) 547-1333. southend@igc.org www.lbbs.org/sep/sep.htm *Non-fiction.*

Thomas Nelson, International Thomas Publishing, Cheriton House, North Way, Andover, ENGLAND SP10 5BE. (01264) 342992, fax (01264) 342788. schools@itps.co.uk www.nelson.co.uk *Publishes* The Caribbean People, *a three-volume illustrated history of the Caribbean appropriate for middle school students.*

Zed Books, c/o St. Martin's Press, Scholarly and Reference Division, 175 Fifth Avenue, New York, NY 10010. (800) 221-7945, fax (212) 777-6359. www.zedbooks.demon.co.uk/home.htm *Nonfiction.*

► **FILMS**

Cinema Guild, 1697 Broadway Suite 506, New York, NY 10019. (212) 246-5522 www.cinemaguild.com

First Run/Icarus Films, 153 Waverly Place, New York, NY 10014. (212) 727-1711, fax (212) 989-7649. info@frif.com www.echonyc.com/~frif/index.html

New Yorker Films, 16 West 61 Street, Floor 11, New York, NY 10023. (212) 247-6110, fax (212) 307-7855. www.newyorkerfilms.com

New Day Films, 22-D Hollywood Avenue, Hohokus, NJ 07432. (888) 367-9154, fax (201) 652-1973.

► **ORGANIZATIONS**

Consulate General of Jamaica
214 King Street West, Suite 402
Toronto, Ontario M5H 3S6, CANADA
(416) 598-3008, fax (416) 598-4928

Council of Caribbean Organizations
8121 Georgia Avenue, NW, #200
Washington, DC 20910

Ecumenical Program on Central America and the Caribbean (EPICA)
1470 Irving Street, NW
Washington, DC 20010
(202) 332-0292
epica@igc.org
www.igc.org/epica

Embassy of Jamaica
Information Section
1520 New Hampshire Avenue, NW
Washington DC 20036
(202) 452-0660
www.caribbean-online.com/jamaica/embassy/washdc

Institute of Jamaica
12 East Street
Kingston, JAMAICA
(876) 922-0620

National Association of Jamaican and Supportive Organizations
630 Lakepointe
Grosse Point Park, MI
(313) 822-9704
www.caribplace.com/hajasolo.htm

Oxfam America
26 West Street
Boston, MA 02111-1206
(800) 77-OXFAM, fax (617) 728-2594
info@oxfamamerica.org

Sistren Theater Collective
20 Kensington Crescent
Kingston 5, JAMAICA
(876) 968-0501 or (876) 929-2457

About the Publishers

ECUMENICAL PROGRAM ON CENTRAL AMERICA AND THE CARIBBEAN (EPICA)

Founded in 1968, EPICA educates the U.S. public about the roots of contemporary problems in the Caribbean, Mexico and Central America. An independent organization working alongside the institutional church, EPICA advocates a joint strategy of change by people in the North and South of the Americas. Through grassroots public education, EPICA serves diverse constituencies working toward a new relationship with the people of the hemisphere. *Programs include:*

■ A small press which **publishes** titles in English and Spanish on the history, politics and culture of Central American and Caribbean countries and Mexico. *The Caribbean: Survival, Struggle and Sovereignty* (1988) is a comprehensive introduction to the region which is widely used as a college text.

■ **Workshops, seminars and speaking tours** on current issues related to U.S. policies in the region. Workshops emphasize participatory learning and critical reflection in small groups.

■ **Study tours** to Central America, Mexico and the Caribbean for church and community groups. Recent groups have visited Jamaica, Puerto Rico, the Dominican Republic, Haiti, Cuba and Mexico, as well as all the Central American nations.

■ *Challenge,* **a journal** of faith and analysis, with Latin American and Caribbean theologians, pastoral workers and social activists.

■ **Information center and library** open to the public.

A non-profit, tax-exempt organization, EPICA is supported by the sale of publications, grants from foundations and religious bodies, and donors.

EPICA, 1470 Irving Street, NW
Washington, DC 20010
(202) 332-0292, fax (202) 332-1184
epica@igc.org ■ www.igc.org/epica

NETWORK OF EDUCATORS ON THE AMERICAS (NECA)

NECA is a nonprofit organization committed to promoting social and economic justice through transformative, quality education for *all* learners. NECA provides opportunities for the development of equitable relationships among families, students, school staff and community members. We believe that these relationships are essential to transform schools so that they are academically rigorous, participatory, culturally affirming, equitable, liberating, connected to the community and respectful of the strengths that people bring to the classroom. *Programs include:*

■ In addition to the *Caribbean Connections* series published with EPICA, over 10 **publications** for use in public schools including the popular *Beyond Heroes and Holidays: A Practical Guide to K-12 Anti-Racist, Multicultural Education and Staff Development.* This interdisciplinary guide offers dozens of lessons and readings.

■ The **Teaching for Change** catalog, the premier source for K-12 classroom materials on critical teaching and school reform. Over 150 books, posters, videos and CDs are featured for all subjects and grade levels. Call for a free copy.

■ In the DC area, the **Tellin' Stories Project** links classrooms and families through bilingual storytelling, quiltmaking and writing. Additionally, NECA co-sponsors the **DC Area Writing Project** (with Howard University and DC Public Schools). Based on the National Writing Project model, the best teachers of writing come together for a 5-week summer institute to read, write, share their knowledge, and become teacher consultants.

■ **Courses and workshops for equity and multicultural education** offer a variety of hands-on programs for in-service settings which address multicultural education from a critical perspective.

NECA, PO Box 73038 Washington, DC 20056
(202) 238-2379 or 429-0137, fax (202) 238-2378
necadc@aol.com ■ www.teachingforchange.org

Caribbean Connections Series

Caribbean Connections: *OVERVIEW OF REGIONAL HISTORY*

❝This book's readings and activities invite students to explore Caribbean history from the inside. It joins the personal and social to tell a powerful story. I wish I'd had this curriculum when I started teaching.❞

— William Bigelow
Social Studies Teacher, Portland Public Schools
Co-editor, Rethinking Columbus

Highlights of OVERVIEW OF REGIONAL HISTORY

- The Arawaks and the Caribs
- The Conquest
- Bitter Sugar
- African Resistance to Slavery
- Emancipation and Free Village Life
- From India to the Caribbean
- The Promise of Education
- Antillean Independence Movements
- Gunboat Diplomacy
- The Cuban Revolution
- West Indian Independence
- Sources of Classroom Materials

Caribbean Connections: *JAMAICA*

❝A superb introduction to Jamaican history and culture: concise, yet accurate and comprehensive. This book is an excellent resource for all school systems which have a serious concern for multicultural education.❞

— E. Leopold Edwards
Council of Caribbean Organizations of the Greater Washington and Baltimore Metropolitan Areas

Highlights of JAMAICA

- Jamaica at a Glance
- A Brief History of Jamaica
- Anansi, Brer Rabbit and the Folk Tradition
- Our Jamaican Heritage
- The Marcus Garvey Movement
- Louise Bennett, National Poetess of Jamaica
- In the Country
- From Rasta to Reggae
- Women's Theater in Jamaica
- Sources of Classroom Materials

Caribbean Connections: *PUERTO RICO*

❝Here are the voices of Puerto Rican workers, women, activists, writers and musicians. Puerto Rican students will find their heritage presented here with knowledge and dignity. Students and teachers of other backgrounds will enjoy a wonderful and informed introduction to Puerto Rican life today.❞

— Dr. Rina Benmayor
Center for Puerto Rican Studies, Hunter College

Highlights of PUERTO RICO

- Puerto Rico at a Glance
- A Brief History of Puerto Rico
- A Lead Box that Couldn't Be Opened*
- Memories of Puerto Rico and New York*
- La Bomba and La Plena, Music of Puerto Rico*
- The Customs and Traditions of the Tabaqueros
- Arturo Alfonso Schomburg
- Our Mothers' Struggle Has Shown Us the Way
- Operation Bootstrap's Legacy
- Vieques and the Navy
- What Future for Puerto Rico?
- Sources of Classroom Materials

* Includes texts in Spanish.

  Caribbean Connections is a project of the Ecumenical Program on Central America and the Caribbean (EPICA) and the Network of Educators on the Americas (NECA). It is funded in part by the D.C. Community Humanities Council, The CarEth Foundation, and the Anita Mishler Education Fund.

Caribbean Connections Series

Caribbean Connections
Teaching about Haiti

Teaching About Haiti is designed to help students fill in the gaps in the news and their textbooks and to provide suggestions for further research. It is designed to help students not only become more informed about Haiti, but also to become involved. We hope that *Teaching about Haiti* helps your students push beyond the traditional boundaries of inquiry into Haiti by bringing the voices and history of Haiti into the classroom.

Highlights of **Teaching about Haiti**

- Haiti's History
- Studying the Media
- Roots of Poverty
- Aristide
- The Roots of Democracy
- Haitian Voices
- Poetry and Folktales
- Songs of Resistance
- Teaching/Action Ideas
- Resource Guide

Caribbean Connections
Moving North

Moving North illuminates the historic ties between the Caribbean and the United States and the diverse reasons that Caribbean people have come north. By presenting the voices of real people from many walks of life, *Moving North* challenges stereotypes and educates students for the task of building an equitable, multicultural society.

Highlights of *Moving North*

- A Primer on Caribbean Migration
- Life Stories
- Fiction, Memoirs and Poetry
- Caribbean Crossroads
- Recommended Reading
- Caribbean Life in Your Community: A Research Guide

To order, send a check, purchase order or VISA/MC number. Postage and handling is $5 for each title, or $8 for two to six titles. For bulk discounts and other information please inquire at (202) 238-2379 or (202) 429-0137. **NECA**, PO Box 73038, Washington, DC 20056, fax: (202) 238-2378 E-mail: necadc@aol.com Make checks payable to NECA.

Please send me:

- ☐   Overview of Regional History $16 (ISBN# 1-878554-06-9)
- ☐   Jamaica $12 (ISBN# 1-878554-05-0)
- ☐   Puerto Rico $12 (ISBN# 1-878554-04-2)
- ☐   Haiti $2 (ISBN# 1-878554-10-7)
- ☐   Moving North $18 (ISBN# 1-878554-12-3)

Name_____

Address_____

City_____ State_____ Zip_____

Phone (h)_____ (w)_____ E-mail_____

Teacher Notes